Company's Coming

®

Soups

Jean Paré

www.companyscoming.com
visit our website

Divider Photo

Vegetable Tortellini Bowl,
   page 147

Props courtesy of: The Bay
                          Winners Stores

We gratefully acknowledge the following suppliers for their
generous support of our Test and Photography Kitchens:

Broil King Barbecues
Corelle®
Hamilton Beach® Canada
Lagostina®
Proctor Silex® Canada
Tupperware®

Table of Contents

Bistro
Favourites

Chowders

Creamed &
Puréed Soups

Healthful
Legumes

Suppertime
Soups

Foreword

Everybody knows a homemade bowl of soup will go a long way in curing whatever ails you. Remember the magical healing powers of Grandma's chicken soup, lovingly administered, when you were in bed with a cold? It wasn't long after that you were back on your feet. And whether it's a hearty chowder, a rich bisque or a cooling gazpacho, all soups contain a little of that same comforting goodness.

In *Soups* you'll find a wide variety of recipes to choose from—sweet to savoury, familiar to exotic, simple to extravagant. And, especially for this book, we've designed a new section called "Grandma's Soups: Her Way & The Easy Way." This section provides you with two variations of three much-loved traditional soups. The first one will reflect the methods Grandma used to make her family favourites, starting from scratch and making stock with leftover or inexpensive turkey, chicken or beef bones. The second version will reflect a quicker and more modern approach, using prepared stock and fast-cooking or precooked meat. (And remember, the stocks from the Grandma's Soups recipes can also be used to make other soups in this book.)

Keep in mind: by making your soups at home, it's easy to make them healthful choices. Reducing the fat in a broth-based soup is as easy as skimming off the fat that collects on the surface. When you're craving a creamy soup but don't want the extra calories, you can create a thick, rich texture by puréeing the vegetables. Try our Roasted Garlic Potato Soup (page 100) and see for yourself. If you're watching your sodium, keep in mind that all the recipes in this book were tested with prepackaged prepared stock. If you want to reduce some of that salt, try using a purchased low-sodium stock or make your own from any of the selections in the Grandma's Soups section. We've also provided an entire section devoted to our high-protein and high-fibre friends—legumes.

So, put your feet up and relax while your soup simmers. Enjoy the aroma and the comforting effect a bowl of homemade soup has on your senses. Flip through this book and let us help you rediscover what you've always known—soups are simply soup-erb!

Jean Paré

Nutrition Information Guidelines

Each recipe has been analyzed using the most up-to-date version of the Canadian Nutrient File from Health Canada, which is based on the United States Department of Agriculture (USDA) Nutrient Data Base. If more than one ingredient is listed (such as "hard margarine or butter"), or a range is given (1 – 2 tsp., 5 – 10 mL), then the first ingredient or amount is used in the analysis. Where an ingredient reads "sprinkle," "optional," or "for garnish", it is not included as part of the nutrition information. Milk, unless stated otherwise, is 1% and cooking oil, unless stated otherwise, is canola.

Margaret Ng, B.Sc. (Hon), M.A.
Registered Dietitian

Tips for Souper Soups

Equipment

The scoop on soup is that you don't need a lot of fancy tools and gizmos to simmer up some savoury fare. Usually, a large cooking pot is all that's required; we used a 4 1/2 quart (4.5 L) **Dutch oven** for most of these recipes.

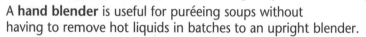

Making stock from scratch, however, calls for a larger vessel to hold the bones, vegetables and liquid. An 8 quart (8 L) **stockpot** is ideal. Not only is it perfect for making the delicious stocks we describe in the Grandma's Soups section, but a stockpot can handle stews, sauces, blanching, boiling and steaming, especially if you're doubling recipes.

A **hand blender** is useful for puréeing soups without having to remove hot liquids in batches to an upright blender.

A **soup skimmer** looks like a large, flat, perforated spoon. It's handy for skimming off foam when you're making the stock, which will prevent it from becoming cloudy.

Small squares of **cheesecloth** and pieces of **string** will allow you to wrap and tie specific herbs and spices into a bundle called a bouquet garni. By tying the other end of your string to your pot handle, you can easily pull out the bouquet garni after cooking.

Souper Servers

A bowl of soup is a warm invitation to any meal, but for special occasions, consider "dressing up" your soup.

- Mugs make a casual statement and are just the thing for around the fire or on the patio. Teacups with matching saucers are elegant vessels for clear broths or consommés. Wineglasses or wide-rimmed "saucer" champagne glasses can handle chilled soups with panache. Or present a frosty soup in a punch bowl and have your guests use the punch glasses to serve themselves.

- Remember to heat your containers when serving hot soup, and chill them for cold soups.

- Tureens come in all colours and shapes and it's fun to play with contrasts, pairing, for example, a blue bowl with a bright orange squash soup. Or get really creative and consider hollowing out a pumpkin or a watermelon for a nature-inspired tureen. And don't forget edible tureens. A hollowed-out bread loaf will make a tasty container for a thick soup.

Double Delicious

Double recipes with no trouble. If you have a larger household or like to make extra soup for freezing, increase your pot size and just double our recipes to reap twice the reward.

Healthy Hints

- Waistline watchers know that soup can make a wonderful, filling meal. To rein in the calories even further, remember to trim the fat off any meat you use, or drain it away if you're searing it first. You can further reduce fat by placing a coffee filter on the soup's surface and blotting it up. Or allow the soup to chill in the refrigerator. The fat will harden on the surface, making it easy to lift out.
- A pot of soup is a great way to use up leftovers, but it's not an opportunity to resurrect suspicious-looking items in the refrigerator. Excellent ingredients make excellent soup, in terms of both flavour and nutrition.

Thickening Tricks

Creamy, rich soups are a feast for the eyes as well as the taste buds. But not all soups are thickened with cream.

A **roux** (pronounced *roo*) is made by heating butter or other fat and sprinkling an equal amount of flour over it. Cook the flour in the fat, then slowly add liquid and stir continuously. When the mixture comes to a boil, reduce the heat. (It's the continual stirring that eliminates the lumps.) Mushrooms, onions or other vegetables are often sautéed in the butter before the flour is added.

A **slurry**, a mixture of cold liquid with flour or cornstarch, can also be used to thicken a soup. Slowly add the slurry to the soup, stirring constantly while bringing it to a boil and then reduce the heat. Over-boiling cornstarch will cause it to separate again. Gently cook roux and slurries several minutes to eliminate the raw taste of flour.

You can also make a **purée** with a portion of the soup and stir it back into the pot for a low-fat creamy texture.

Freezer Facts

- Freeze homemade stock in different sizes to flavour not just soups but gravies, sauces, polenta and other dishes. For tiny amounts, freeze stock in ice cube trays, then transfer the cubes to a plastic freezer bag.
- Use airtight containers to reduce freezer burn.
- Freeze small batches of soup efficiently by placing good-quality freezer bags inside clean milk cartons and filling the bags. Seal the bags and freeze. When the contents are frozen, remove the milk carton to use again, and neatly stack the labelled soup bricks against the freezer wall.
- Certain ingredients, specifically potatoes and pasta, do not freeze well. Consider adding these ingredients after thawing. Undercook rice before freezing, as it will soften.
- Soups thickened with dairy products, flour or cornstarch may separate when frozen. Whisk the soup while heating it to allow it to blend together again.
- Garnishes of yogurt, sour cream and mayonnaise do not freeze well. Add these just before serving.

Grandma's Turkey Soup

Remember Christmas dinner at Grandma's? As soon as the turkey was carved the bones would be simmering on the stovetop to make the stock for her turkey soup. Grandma could find value in anything—even turkey bones!

TURKEY STOCK

Leftover turkey carcass	1	1
Cold water	18 cups	4.5 L
Celery ribs, with leaves, halved	6	6
Medium onion, halved	1	1
Medium carrot, halved	1	1
Garlic clove	1	1
Bay leaf	1	1
Whole black peppercorns	10	10

SOUP

Water	1 1/2 cups	375 mL
Short grain white rice	1 cup	250 mL
Chopped onion	1 cup	250 mL
Chopped celery	1 cup	250 mL
Chopped fresh (or frozen) green beans	1 cup	250 mL
Diced carrot	1 cup	250 mL
Diced peeled potato	1 cup	250 mL
Parsley flakes	1 tbsp.	15 mL
Salt	2 tsp.	10 mL
Pepper	1/2 tsp.	2 mL
Dried thyme	1/2 tsp.	2 mL
Dried sage	1/2 tsp.	2 mL
Chopped cooked turkey	2 cups	500 mL
Half-and-half cream (optional)	1/2 cup	125 mL

Turkey Stock: Break up turkey carcass to fit in large pot. Add first amount of water. Bring to a boil. Boil, uncovered, for 5 minutes without stirring. Skim and discard foam from side of pot.

Add next 6 ingredients. Stir. Reduce heat to medium-low. Simmer, partially covered, for about 3 hours, stirring occasionally, until turkey falls off bones. Remove from heat. Discard larger bones. Strain stock through sieve into separate large pot. Discard solids. Makes about 11 cups (2.75 L) stock.

(continued on next page)

Soup: Add next 12 ingredients to stock in pot. Bring to a boil. Reduce heat to medium-low. Simmer, partially covered, for about 30 minutes, stirring occasionally, until vegetables and rice are tender.

Add turkey and cream. Cook for about 5 minutes, stirring occasionally, until heated through. Makes about 14 cups (3.5 L).

1 cup (250 mL): 108 Calories; 0.7 g Total Fat (0.2 g Mono, 0.2 g Poly, 0.2 g Sat); 20 mg Cholesterol; 17 g Carbohydrate; 1 g Fibre; 8 g Protein; 370 mg Sodium

Easy Turkey Soup

Truth be known, not everyone has turkey bones at the ready when they're hankerin' for some turkey soup. Not to worry, if you have ground turkey and chicken broth, you still can still sup on a delightful turkey soup.

Cooking oil	1 tbsp.	15 mL
Lean ground turkey	3/4 lb.	340 g
Chopped onion	3/4 cup	175 mL
Chopped celery	3/4 cup	175 mL
All-purpose flour	2 tsp.	10 mL
Chicken stock	8 cups	2 L
Frozen mixed vegetables	2 cups	500 mL
Frozen diced hash brown potatoes	1 cup	250 mL
Very small pasta (such as orzo or alphabet)	2/3 cup	150 mL
Parsley flakes	2 tsp.	10 mL
Poultry seasoning	1/2 tsp.	2 mL
Pepper	1/4 tsp.	1 mL
Half-and-half cream (optional)	1/2 cup	125 mL

Heat cooking oil in large saucepan on medium-high. Add next 3 ingredients. Scramble-fry for about 10 minutes until vegetables are softened and turkey is no longer pink.

Sprinkle with flour. Heat and stir for 1 minute.

Add next 7 ingredients. Bring to a boil. Reduce heat to medium-low. Simmer, partially covered, for about 15 minutes, stirring occasionally, until pasta and vegetables are tender.

Add cream. Heat and stir for about 1 minute until heated through. Makes about 10 cups (2.5 L).

1 cup (250 mL): 156 Calories; 5.0 g Total Fat (1.9 g Mono, 1.3 g Poly, 1.3 g Sat); 27 mg Cholesterol; 18 g Carbohydrate; 1 g Fibre; 10 g Protein; 739 mg Sodium

Grandma's Beef Barley Soup

Waste not, want not, Grandma always used to say. It was the beef bones that made Grandma's beef stock so rich and savoury. And Grandma, as usual, had another trick up her sleeve—she knew that a long simmering time really brought out the flavour in her beef barley soup.

BEEF STOCK

Beef neck bones	3 lbs.	1.4 kg
Bone-in beef shanks	1 lb.	454 g
Cold water	16 cups	4 L
Celery ribs, with leaves, halved	6	6
Medium onions, halved	2	2
Medium carrot, halved	1	1
Bay leaves	2	2
Whole black peppercorns	10	10

SOUP

Diced peeled potato	2 cups	500 mL
Can of condensed tomato soup	10 oz.	284 mL
Chopped onion	1 cup	250 mL
Chopped celery	1 cup	250 mL
Diced carrot	1 cup	250 mL
Diced parsnip (optional)	1 cup	250 mL
Pearl barley	2/3 cup	150 mL
Salt	1 tsp.	5 mL
Pepper	3/4 tsp.	4 mL

Beef Stock: Put first 3 ingredients into large pot. Bring to a boil. Boil, uncovered, for 5 minutes without stirring. Skim and discard foam from side of pot.

Add next 5 ingredients. Stir. Reduce heat to medium-low. Simmer, partially covered, for about 4 hours, stirring occasionally, until beef starts to fall off bones. Remove from heat. Remove bones and shanks to cutting board using slotted spoon. Remove beef from bones. Discard bones. Chop beef coarsely. Set aside. Strain stock through sieve into separate large pot. Discard solids. Makes about 10 cups (2.5 L) stock.

(continued on next page)

Soup: Add remaining 9 ingredients to stock in pot. Bring to a boil. Add beef. Reduce heat to medium-low. Simmer, partially covered, for about 45 minutes, stirring occasionally, until barley and vegetables are tender. Makes about 14 cups (3.5 L).

1 cup (250 mL): 112 Calories; 2.1 g Total Fat (0.8 g Mono, 0.3 g Poly, 0.7 g Sat); 11 mg Cholesterol; 17 g Carbohydrate; 2 g Fibre; 6 g Protein; 345 mg Sodium

Easy Beef Barley Soup

OK, so perhaps you're the type who would like to leave the bones at the butcher's. But that doesn't mean you would ever sacrifice quality. No bones about it, using prepared stock and ground beef enables you to serve up an absolutely delicious fresh vegetable and beef barley soup in a fraction of the time.

Cooking oil	2 tsp.	10 mL
Extra-lean ground beef	1/2 lb.	225 g
Sliced fresh white mushrooms	1/2 cup	125 mL
Chopped onion	1/2 cup	125 mL
Chopped celery	1/2 cup	125 mL
All-purpose flour	2 tsp.	10 mL
Beef stock	6 cups	1.5 L
Sliced carrot	1 cup	250 mL
Chopped peeled potato	1 cup	250 mL
Pearl barley	1/3 cup	75 mL
Tomato paste (see Tip, page 49)	2 tbsp.	30 mL
Pepper	1/4 tsp.	1 mL
Can of evaporated milk	5 1/2 oz.	160 mL

Heat cooking oil in large saucepan on medium. Add next 4 ingredients. Scramble-fry for about 10 minutes until beef is no longer pink.

Sprinkle with flour. Heat and stir for 1 minute.

Add next 6 ingredients. Bring to a boil. Reduce heat to medium-low. Simmer, partially covered, for about 1 hour, stirring occasionally, until barley and vegetables are tender and soup is thickened.

Add evaporated milk. Heat and stir for 1 to 2 minutes until heated through. Makes about 7 cups (1.75 L).

1 cup (250 mL): 186 Calories; 6.3 g Total Fat (2.6 g Mono, 0.7 g Poly, 2.4 g Sat); 23 mg Cholesterol; 20 g Carbohydrate; 2 g Fibre; 12 g Protein; 793 mg Sodium

Grandma's Chicken Noodle Soup

*Grandma always could cure whatever ailed you. Whether she used
a hug or some of her long-simmered, made-from-scratch chicken soup,
you always left her place feeling better about the world.*

CHICKEN STOCK

Bone-in chicken parts (see Note)	4 lbs.	1.8 kg
Water	10 cups	2.5 L
Celery ribs, with leaves, halved	2	2
Large onion, quartered	1	1
Large carrot, halved	1	1
Sprigs of fresh thyme	3	3
Sprig of fresh parsley	1	1
Bay leaves	2	2
Garlic clove	1	1
Whole black peppercorns	12	12

SOUP

Cooking oil	2 tsp.	10 mL
Chopped onion	1/2 cup	125 mL
Chopped carrot	1/2 cup	125 mL
Chopped celery	1/2 cup	125 mL
Spaghetti, broken into about 3 inch (7.5 cm) pieces	3 oz.	85 g
Chopped fresh parsley	1/4 cup	60 mL
Salt	3/4 tsp.	4 mL
Pepper	1/4 tsp.	1 mL

Chicken Stock: Put chicken and water into Dutch oven or large pot. Bring to a boil. Boil, uncovered, for 5 minutes without stirring. Skim and discard foam from side of pot.

Add next 8 ingredients. Stir. Bring to a boil. Reduce heat to medium-low. Simmer, uncovered, for about 3 hours, stirring occasionally, until chicken is tender and starts to fall off bones. Remove from heat. Remove chicken and bones to cutting board using slotted spoon. Remove chicken from bones. Discard bones. Chop enough chicken to make 2 cups (500 mL). Reserve remaining chicken for another use. Strain stock through sieve into large bowl. Discard solids. Skim fat from stock (see Healthy Hints, page 9). Makes about 6 1/2 cups (1.6 L) stock.

(continued on next page)

Soup: Heat cooking oil in large saucepan on medium. Add next 3 ingredients. Cook for 5 to 10 minutes, stirring often, until onion is softened. Add stock. Bring to a boil.

Add spaghetti. Cook, uncovered, for about 10 minutes, stirring occasionally, until spaghetti and vegetables are tender.

Add chicken and remaining 3 ingredients. Heat and stir until chicken is heated through. Makes about 7 1/2 cups (1.9 L).

1 cup (250 mL): 137 Calories; 4.3 g Total Fat (1.8 g Mono, 1.1 g Poly, 0.9 g Sat); 34 mg Cholesterol; 11 g Carbohydrate; 1 g Fibre; 13 g Protein; 287 mg Sodium

Pictured on page 17.

Note: Use whichever cuts of chicken you prefer as long as the weight used is equal to that listed.

Easy Chicken Noodle Soup

You're no slouch in the caring department either. Some may say you've got a trick up your sleeve that Grandma might not have thought of—you use prepared stock and cooked chicken, so you can get your healing chicken noodle soup to those in need in less than 25 minutes!

Chicken stock	4 cups	1 L
Dried thyme	1/4 tsp.	1 mL
Garlic powder	1/4 tsp.	1 mL
Bay leaf	1	1
Frozen mixed vegetables	1 cup	250 mL
Diced cooked chicken	1 cup	250 mL
Cooked spaghetti, coarsely chopped	1 cup	250 mL
Pepper	1/4 tsp.	1 mL
Chopped green onion	1/2 cup	125 mL

Combine first 4 ingredients in large saucepan. Bring to a boil.

Add next 4 ingredients. Cook for about 5 minutes, stirring occasionally, until heated through. Discard bay leaf.

Add green onion. Stir. Makes about 5 cups (1.25 L).

1 cup (250 mL): 118 Calories; 2.7 g Total Fat (0.8 g Mono, 0.6 g Poly, 1.0 g Sat); 24 mg Cholesterol; 12 g Carbohydrate; 1 g Fibre; 11 g Protein; 718 mg Sodium

Pictured on page 17.

Tomato Noodle Soup

Kids of all ages will clamour to the table. Soup's on! (In less than 30 minutes.)

Cooking oil	1/2 tsp.	2 mL
Finely chopped onion	1/2 cup	125 mL
Finely chopped carrot	1/4 cup	60 mL
Chicken stock	3 cups	750 mL
Can of diced tomatoes (with juice)	14 oz.	398 mL
Can of vegetable cocktail juice	10 oz.	284 mL
Water	1 cup	250 mL
Granulated sugar	2 tsp.	10 mL
Dried oregano	1/2 tsp.	2 mL
Dried basil	1/2 tsp.	2 mL
Pepper	1/8 tsp.	0.5 mL
Spaghettini, broken up	1 3/4 oz.	50 g

Heat cooking oil in large saucepan on medium-high. Add onion and carrot. Cook for 1 to 2 minutes, stirring often, until vegetables start to brown.

Add next 8 ingredients. Stir. Cover. Bring to a boil.

Add spaghettini. Stir. Reduce heat to medium. Boil gently, partially covered, for 10 to 12 minutes, stirring occasionally, until pasta is tender but firm. Makes about 7 cups (1.75 L).

1 cup (250 mL): 64 Calories; 0.9 g Total Fat (0.2 g Mono, 0.2 g Poly, 0.3 g Sat); 0 mg Cholesterol; 12 g Carbohydrate; 1 g Fibre; 2 g Protein; 616 mg Sodium

1. Easy Chicken Noodle Soup, page 15
2. Grandma's Chicken Noodle Soup, page 14

Props courtesy of: Pfaltzgraff Canada

Brothy Bests

Vegetable Soup

A healthy, delicately seasoned tomato-based soup. An easy recipe to double or even triple. Freeze any extra so you'll have something delicious to serve when hungry company comes knocking at the door.

Water	2 1/2 cups	625 mL
Chopped onion	3/4 cup	175 mL
Diced carrot	3/4 cup	175 mL
Diced peeled potato	3/4 cup	175 mL
Diced yellow turnip	1/4 cup	60 mL
Diced celery, with leaves	1/4 cup	60 mL
Bay leaf	1	1
Granulated sugar	1/4 tsp.	1 mL
Salt	1 tsp.	5 mL
Pepper	1/8 tsp.	0.5 mL
Ground thyme	1/8 tsp.	0.5 mL
Tomato juice	1 cup	250 mL
Vegetable bouillon powder	1 tsp.	5 mL

Combine first 11 ingredients in large saucepan. Bring to a boil. Reduce heat to medium-low. Simmer, covered, for about 20 minutes, stirring occasionally, until vegetables are tender. Discard bay leaf.

Add tomato juice and bouillon powder. Stir. Simmer, uncovered, for about 5 minutes until heated through. Makes about 5 cups (1.25 L).

1 cup (250 mL): 54 Calories; 0.2 g Total Fat (trace Mono, 0.1 g Poly, 0.1 g Sat); trace Cholesterol; 12 g Carbohydrate; 2 g Fibre; 2 g Protein; 808 mg Sodium

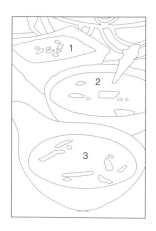

1. Gingered Carrot Soup, page 85
2. Minted Green Pea Chowder, page 73
3. Roasted Beet And Greens Soup, page 22

Props courtesy of: Danesco Inc.
　　　　　　　　　The Dazzling Gourmet
　　　　　　　　　Canhome Global

Mexican Citrus Soup

Mas sopa, por favor! (More soup please!) So aromatic and refreshing, you will ask for more. *Factor in extra time for roasting the garlic and onion.*

Garlic bulb	1	1
Medium onion (with skin), halved	1	1
Corn tortillas (6 inch, 15 cm, diameter)	2	2
Cooking spray		
Cooking oil	1 tsp.	5 mL
Chopped onion	1 cup	250 mL
Chicken stock	4 cups	1 L
Water	1 cup	250 mL
Diced fresh tomato	2 cups	500 mL
Small jalapeño pepper, seeds and ribs removed, finely diced (see Tip, page 26)	1	1
Dried oregano	1/4 tsp.	1 mL
Ground cumin	1/4 tsp.	1 mL
Grated lime zest	1/2 tsp.	2 mL
Grated orange zest	1/2 tsp.	2 mL
Grated grapefruit zest	1/2 tsp.	2 mL
Juice from 2 medium limes		
Juice from 1 medium orange		
Juice from 1 medium grapefruit		
Salt	1/2 tsp.	2 mL
Pepper	1/4 tsp.	1 mL

Chopped fresh cilantro, for garnish

Trim 1/4 inch (6 mm) from garlic bulb to expose tops of cloves, leaving bulb intact. Wrap loosely in greased foil. Place on ungreased baking sheet. Place onion halves, cut side down on same baking sheet. Bake in 375°F (190°C) oven for about 45 minutes until garlic and onion are softened. Let stand until cool enough to handle. Squeeze garlic bulb to remove cloves from peel. Discard peel. Discard skins from onion. Chop onion. Set aside.

Spray tortillas with cooking spray. Heat small frying pan on medium-high. Cook tortillas for 1 to 2 minutes per side until crisp and browned. Transfer to cutting board. Cut into 1/4 inch (6 mm) wide strips while warm. Set aside.

(continued on next page)

Brothy Bests

Heat cooking oil in large saucepan on medium. Add second amount of onion. Cook for about 5 to 10 minutes, stirring often, until softened.

Add next 6 ingredients. Add roasted garlic and onion. Stir. Bring to a boil. Reduce heat to medium-low. Simmer, covered, for 10 minutes to blend flavours.

Add next 8 ingredients. Cook for 2 minutes to blend flavours. Makes about 9 cups (2.25 L).

Sprinkle cilantro and tortilla strips on individual servings. Serves 6.

1 serving: 127 Calories; 1.9 g Total Fat (0.6 g Mono, 0.6 g Poly, 0.5 g Sat); 0 mg Cholesterol; 26 g Carbohydrate; 3 g Fibre; 4 g Protein; 797 mg Sodium

Pictured on page 125.

Tomato Fennel Soup

Fennel, tomato and a lingering pepper finish make this stylish soup an artful choice.

Cooking oil	2 tsp.	10 mL
Chopped fennel bulb (white part only)	2 cups	500 mL
Chopped onion	1 cup	250 mL
Garlic cloves, minced (or 1/2 tsp., 2 mL, powder)	2	2
Can of diced tomatoes (with juice)	28 oz.	796 mL
Chicken stock	2 cups	500 mL
Balsamic vinegar	2 tsp.	10 mL
Granulated sugar	1 tsp.	5 mL
Salt	1/2 tsp.	2 mL
Pepper	1/4 tsp.	1 mL

Heat cooking oil in large saucepan on medium. Add next 3 ingredients. Cook for about 10 minutes, stirring often, until onion and fennel are softened.

Add remaining 6 ingredients. Stir. Bring to a boil. Reduce heat to medium-low. Simmer, partially covered, for about 20 minutes, stirring occasionally, until fennel is tender. Carefully process in blender until smooth (see Safety Tip). Makes about 6 cups (1.5 L).

1 cup (250 mL): 71 Calories; 2.1 g Total Fat (1.0 g Mono, 0.6 g Poly, 0.3 g Sat); 0 mg Cholesterol; 12 g Carbohydrate; 2 g Fibre; 3 g Protein; 720 mg Sodium

Safety Tip: Follow blender manufacturer's instructions for processing hot liquids.

Roasted Beet And Greens Soup

Highlighted with tangy balsamic vinegar and fresh dill,
you just can't beat these sweet roasted beets! Roasting whole
vegetables takes a bit of time but the flavour is worth it.

Medium beets, scrubbed clean and trimmed	1 lb.	454 g
Small onion (with skin)	1	1
Chicken (or vegetable) stock	4 cups	1 L
Fresh spinach (or beet) leaves, lightly packed, cut into thin strips	2 cups	500 mL
Pepper	1/4 tsp.	1 mL
Balsamic vinegar	1 – 2 tbsp.	15 – 30 mL
Chopped fresh dill (or 1/2 tsp., 2 mL, dill weed)	2 tsp.	10 mL

Wrap each beet and onion individually in foil. Bake directly on rack in centre of 375°F (190°C) oven for about 1 1/2 hours until tender. Remove foil. Let stand until cool enough to handle. Peel beets (see Tip) and onion. Grate beets. Finely chop onion. Set aside.

Bring stock to a boil in large saucepan. Add spinach, pepper, beets and onion. Cook, uncovered, for about 5 minutes, stirring occasionally, until vegetables are heated through.

Add vinegar and dill. Stir. Makes about 5 1/2 cups (1.4 L).

1 cup (250 mL): 49 Calories; 0.6 g Total Fat (trace Mono, 0.1 g Poly, 0.4 g Sat); 0 mg Cholesterol; 9 g Carbohydrate; 1.9 g Fibre; 3 g Protein; 685 mg Sodium

Pictured on page 18.

 tip Don't get caught red handed! Wear rubber gloves when handling beets.

Eggplant And Tomato Soup

You can almost feel the warmth of the Tuscan sun as you
savour the flavour of this smooth and sophisticated soup.

Olive oil	2 tbsp.	30 mL
Chopped eggplant (with peel)	2 cups	500 mL
Chopped onion	1 cup	250 mL
Salt	1/8 tsp.	0.5 mL
Garlic clove, minced (or 1/4 tsp., 1 mL, powder)	1	1
Tomato paste (see Tip, page 49)	1 tbsp.	15 mL
Vegetable (or chicken) stock	4 cups	1 L
Can of plum tomatoes (with juice)	14 oz.	398 mL
Bay leaf	1	1
Dried oregano	1/2 tsp.	2 mL

Heat olive oil in large saucepan on medium-high. Add next 3 ingredients. Cook for about 5 minutes, stirring often, until onion is softened.

Add garlic. Heat and stir for about 1 minute until fragrant.

Add tomato paste. Heat and stir for 1 minute.

Add remaining 4 ingredients. Stir. Bring to a boil. Reduce heat to medium-low. Simmer, covered, for 15 minutes, stirring occasionally, to blend flavours. Discard bay leaf. Carefully process with hand blender or in blender until smooth (see Safety Tip). Makes about 7 cups (1.75 L).

1 cup (250 mL): 74 Calories; 4.5 g Total Fat (2.9 g Mono, 0.4 g Poly, 0.9 g Sat); 0 mg Cholesterol; 8 g Carbohydrate; 2 g Fibre; 2 g Protein; 632 mg Sodium

Safety Tip: Follow blender manufacturer's instructions for processing hot liquids.

Paré Pointer
You can always make a hot dog stand—just steal his chair.

Daydreams Of Summer Soup

Enjoy this autumn-orange soup as the lazy days of summer draw to a close and the garden harvest thrives. Roasting the vegetables lends a mellow blending of flavours.

Large tomatoes, quartered	2 lbs.	900 g
Medium zucchini (with peel), cut crosswise into 8 pieces	1	1
Large red pepper, halved	1	1
Unpeeled garlic cloves	2	2
Olive (or cooking) oil	1 tbsp.	15 mL
Salt, sprinkle		
Pepper, sprinkle		
Olive (or cooking) oil	2 tsp.	10 mL
Chopped onion	1 1/2 cups	375 mL
Chopped celery	1/2 cup	125 mL
Chicken stock	4 cups	1 L
Dried basil	1/4 tsp.	1 mL
Dried rosemary, crushed, just a pinch		

Put first 4 ingredients into extra large bowl. Drizzle with first amount of olive oil. Toss until coated. Arrange, peel side down, in single layer on ungreased baking sheet with sides. Sprinkle with salt and pepper. Bake in 450°F (230°C) oven for about 30 minutes until vegetables are softened and starting to brown on bottom. Transfer red pepper halves to small bowl. Cover with plastic wrap. Let sweat for about 15 minutes until cool enough to handle. Remove and discard skins. Squeeze garlic to remove cloves from peel. Discard peels. Remove and discard skins from tomatoes. Set aside.

Heat second amount of olive oil in Dutch oven on medium. Add onion and celery. Cook for about 5 to 10 minutes, stirring often, until softened.

Add remaining 3 ingredients. Add roasted vegetables and any accumulated liquid. Bring to a boil. Reduce heat to medium-low. Simmer, covered, for 20 minutes, stirring occasionally, to blend flavours. Carefully process with hand blender or in blender until no large pieces remain (see Safety Tip). Makes about 8 cups (2 L).

1 cup (250 mL): 86 Calories; 3.7 g Total Fat (2.2 g Mono, 0.5 g Poly, 0.7 g Sat); 0 mg Cholesterol; 13 g Carbohydrate; 3 g Fibre; 3 g Protein; 449 mg Sodium

Safety Tip: Follow blender manufacturer's instructions for processing hot liquids.

Egg Drop Soup

Here's a full-flavoured chicken soup with an Asian influence.
We used mirin, a popular Japanese cooking ingredient,
to make the taste truly authentic.

Chicken stock	6 cups	1.5 L
Mirin (see Note)	2 tbsp.	30 mL
Sesame oil (optional)	1 tsp.	5 mL
Piece of ginger root (1 inch, 2.5 cm, length), sliced	1	1
Garlic cloves, lightly crushed	2	2
Pepper	1/4 tsp.	1 mL
Green onions, white parts only, green parts reserved	2	2
Large eggs	2	2
Mirin (see Note)	2 tsp.	10 mL

Reserved green onion, finely chopped

Combine first 7 ingredients in large saucepan. Bring to a boil. Reduce heat to medium. Boil gently, uncovered, for 10 minutes to blend flavours. Remove and discard ginger, garlic and white parts of onion. Reduce heat to low.

Beat eggs and second amount of mirin with fork in small cup until smooth. Gradually add to broth, stirring constantly, until fine egg threads form. Do not boil. Remove from heat.

Sprinkle reserved green onion on individual servings. Makes about 5 1/2 cups (1.4 L).

1 cup (250 mL): 62 Calories; 3.2 g Total Fat (1.0 g Mono, 0.6 g Poly, 1.2 g Sat); 78 mg Cholesterol; 4 g Carbohydrate; trace Fibre; 4 g Protein; 960 mg Sodium

Note: Mirin is a Japanese sweet cooking rice wine. It is available in specialty Asian grocery stores.

Variation: For a spicier soup, mince the garlic cloves instead of using crushed and use 1 tbsp. (15 mL) finely grated gingerroot instead of slices. Do not strain.

Tomato Gin Soup

A tipple of gin adds a cheeky flair to this fresh lime and tomato soup.

Cooking oil	1 tsp.	5 mL
Chopped onion	1 cup	250 mL
Chopped celery	1/2 cup	125 mL
Garlic clove, minced (or 1/4 tsp., 1 mL, powder)	1	1
Jalapeño pepper, seeds and ribs removed, finely diced (see Tip)	1	1
Tomato juice	4 cups	1 L
Can of diced tomatoes (with juice)	14 oz.	398 mL
Water	1 1/2 cups	375 mL
Worcestershire sauce	1 tbsp.	15 mL
Grated lime zest	1 tsp.	5 mL
Gin	1/3 cup	75 mL
Lime juice	1/4 cup	60 mL
Liquid honey	1 tbsp.	15 mL

Heat cooking oil in large saucepan on medium. Add next 4 ingredients. Cook for 5 to 10 minutes, stirring often, until onion and celery are softened.

Add next 5 ingredients. Bring to a boil. Reduce heat to medium-low. Simmer, partially covered, for about 15 minutes, stirring occasionally, until vegetables are tender. Carefully process with hand blender or in blender until smooth (see Safety Tip).

Add remaining 3 ingredients. Stir. Makes about 8 cups (2 L).

1 cup (250 mL): 83 Calories; 0.8 g Total Fat (0.4 g Mono, 0.3 g Poly, 0.1 g Sat); 0 mg Cholesterol; 14 g Carbohydrate; 2 g Fibre; 2 g Protein; 579 mg Sodium

Safety Tip: Follow blender manufacturer's instructions for processing hot liquids.

 Hot peppers contain capsaicin in the seeds and ribs. Removing the seeds and ribs will reduce the heat. Wear rubber gloves when handling hot peppers and avoid touching your eyes. Wash your hands well afterwards.

Chicken Asparagus Soup

Don't spare the asparagus! This soup is an asparagus-lover's dream come true. If you prefer your asparagus fresh, try the variation.

Cooking oil	2 tsp.	10 mL
Chopped onion	1 cup	250 mL
Chopped celery	1 cup	250 mL
Chicken stock	4 cups	1 L
Grated carrot	1/4 cup	60 mL
Dried tarragon	1/2 tsp.	2 mL
Garlic powder	1/4 tsp.	1 mL
Pepper	1/4 tsp.	1 mL
Diced cooked chicken	1 1/2 cups	375 mL
Can of asparagus tips (with liquid), cut into 1/2 inch (12 mm) pieces	12 oz.	341 mL

Heat cooking oil in large saucepan on medium. Add onion and celery. Cook for 5 to 10 minutes, stirring often, until onion is softened.

Add next 5 ingredients. Bring to a boil. Reduce heat to medium. Boil gently, partially covered, for 5 minutes until carrot is softened.

Add chicken and asparagus tips with liquid. Cook, stirring occasionally, for about 3 minutes until chicken is heated through. Makes about 6 1/2 cups (1.6 L).

1 cup (250 mL): 108 Calories; 4.3 g Total Fat (1.7 g Mono, 1.1 g Poly, 1.1 g Sat); 29 mg Cholesterol; 5.8 g Carbohydrate; 1 g Fibre; 12 g Protein; 764 mg Sodium

SPRING ASPARAGUS SOUP: Use 1 cup (250 mL) chopped fresh asparagus instead of canned asparagus. Increase the chicken stock to 4 2/3 cups (1.15 L). Cook asparagus until tender.

Paré Pointer
He's no quitter. So far he's been fired from every job.

Brothy Bests

Spring Saffron Soup

*Saffron lends a unique colour and taste to this enchanting soup.
Even though saffron is the world's most expensive spice, a very little goes
a long way in imparting taste and flavour. In a pinch? Forgo the saffron
and substitute turmeric for the same vibrant colour.*

Cooking oil	2 tsp.	10 mL
Chopped onion	1 cup	250 mL
Chopped carrot	3/4 cup	175 mL
Chopped celery	1/2 cup	125 mL
Salt	1/4 tsp.	1 mL
Chicken stock	5 cups	1.25 L
Saffron threads	1/8 tsp.	0.5 mL
Bay leaf	1	1
Orzo	1/3 cup	75 mL
Fresh asparagus, trimmed of tough ends, cut into 1 inch (2.5 cm) pieces	1 lb.	454 g
Frozen uncooked shrimp (peeled and deveined), thawed and chopped	1/2 lb.	225 g

Grated Parmesan cheese, for garnish

Heat cooking oil in large saucepan on medium. Add next 4 ingredients. Cook for 5 to 10 minutes, stirring often, until onion is softened.

Add next 3 ingredients. Stir. Bring to a boil. Add orzo. Stir. Reduce heat to medium. Boil gently, uncovered, for 5 minutes.

Add asparagus. Stir. Cook for 3 to 5 minutes until asparagus is tender-crisp.

Add shrimp. Heat and stir for about 2 minutes until shrimp turn pink. Discard bay leaf.

Garnish individual servings with Parmesan cheese. Makes about 7 1/2 cups (1.9 L).

1 cup (250 mL): 110 Calories; 2.4 g Total Fat (0.8 g Mono, 0.7 g Poly, 0.6 g Sat); 46 mg Cholesterol; 13 g Carbohydrate; 2 g Fibre; 10 g Protein; 709 mg Sodium

Lemony Chicken Rice Soup

If lemon chicken is one of your favourite dishes, you'll
find the same tangy flavours in this delightful soup.

Cooking oil	1 tbsp.	15 mL
Boneless, skinless chicken breast halves, cut in half lengthwise and cut crosswise into thin strips	3/4 lb.	340 g
Chopped onion	1 cup	250 mL
Thinly sliced carrot	1 cup	250 mL
Garlic clove, minced (or 1/4 tsp., 1 mL, powder)	1	1
Chicken stock	5 cups	1.25 L
Long grain white rice	1/4 cup	60 mL
Grated lemon zest	1 tsp.	5 mL
Fresh spinach leaves, lightly packed, chopped	2 cups	500 mL
Lemon juice	2 tbsp.	30 mL

Heat cooking oil in large saucepan on medium-high. Add chicken. Cook for about 4 minutes, stirring often, until no longer pink. Remove chicken to plate using slotted spoon.

Reduce heat to medium. Add next 3 ingredients. Cook for about 10 minutes, scraping any brown bits from bottom of pan, until onion and carrot start to soften.

Add next 3 ingredients. Add chicken. Bring to a boil. Reduce heat to medium-low. Simmer, partially covered, for about 20 minutes, stirring occasionally, until rice is tender.

Add spinach and lemon juice. Stir. Cook for about 5 minutes, stirring occasionally, until spinach is wilted. Makes about 7 1/2 cups (1.9 L).

1 cup (250 mL): 125 Calories; 3.1 g Total Fat (1.3 g Mono, 0.8 g Poly, 0.7 g Sat); 26 mg Cholesterol; 12 g Carbohydrate; 1 g Fibre; 13 g Protein; 600 mg Sodium

Mushroom Wild Rice Broth

Who isn't wild for wild rice and mushrooms? A fresh light broth
surrounds chewy wild rice, sweet peas and soft earthy mushrooms.

Water	2 cups	500 mL
Wild rice	1/2 cup	125 mL
Salt	1/2 tsp.	2 mL
Cooking oil	1 tsp.	5 mL
Chopped onion	1 cup	250 mL
Garlic clove, minced (or 1/4 tsp., 1 mL, powder)	1	1
Sliced fresh white mushrooms	4 cups	1 L
Beef stock	4 cups	1 L
Water	1 cup	250 mL
Chopped fresh thyme (or 1/4 tsp., 1 mL, dried)	1 tsp.	5 mL
Frozen peas	1 cup	250 mL

Combine first 3 ingredients in small saucepan. Bring to a boil. Reduce heat to medium-low. Cook, covered, for about 30 minutes until almost tender. Remove from heat. Let stand for about 30 minutes until tender. Drain. Set aside.

Heat cooking oil in large saucepan on medium. Add onion and garlic. Cook for 5 to 10 minutes, stirring often, until onion is softened.

Add mushrooms. Cook for about 5 minutes, stirring often, until mushrooms release liquid.

Add next 3 ingredients and wild rice. Bring to a boil.

Add peas. Stir. Cook for 1 to 2 minutes until peas are tender. Makes about 7 cups (1.75 L).

1 cup (250 mL): 95 Calories; 1.1 g Total Fat (0.4 g Mono, 0.4 g Poly, 0.1 g Sat); 0 mg Cholesterol; 16 g Carbohydrate; 3 g Fibre; 6 g Protein; 678 mg Sodium

Brothy Bests

Tomato Beef Soup

Tuh-MAY-toh, tuh-MAH-toh, no matter how you say it, the
simple flavours of this fast and easy treat will appeal to all.

Cooking oil	2 tsp.	10 mL
Diced carrot	1 cup	250 mL
Finely chopped onion	1/2 cup	125 mL
Diced celery	1/3 cup	75 mL
Beef stock	3 cups	750 mL
Diced peeled potato	2 1/3 cups	575 mL
Tomato juice	2 cups	500 mL
Cooked (or deli) roast beef slices, cut into thin strips (about 2/3 cup, 150 mL)	1/4 lb.	113 g
Bay leaf	1	1
Worcestershire sauce	1 tsp.	5 mL
Salt	1 tsp.	5 mL
Pepper	1/8 tsp.	0.5 mL
Frozen peas	1 cup	250 mL

Heat cooking oil in large saucepan on medium. Add next 3 ingredients. Cook for 5 to 10 minutes, stirring often, until onion is softened.

Add next 8 ingredients. Stir. Bring to a boil. Reduce heat to medium-low. Simmer, covered, for 20 to 25 minutes, stirring occasionally, until potato is tender. Discard bay leaf.

Add peas. Stir. Simmer, uncovered, for about 3 minutes until peas are tender. Makes about 8 cups (2 L).

1 cup (250 mL): 127 Calories; 3.3 g Total Fat (1.5 g Mono, 0.5 g Poly, 0.9 g Sat); 9 mg Cholesterol; 17 g Carbohydrate; 3 g Fibre; 8 g Protein; 897 mg Sodium

Miso Soup With Noodles

*Miso is the basis for many tasty Japanese dishes. It comes in several
varieties—the lighter the colour, the more delicate the taste. Although you
can use any variety of miso, we went all out and used red miso because
the stronger flavour combines well with the hot chili. For those who
like a saltier flavour, serve soy sauce on the side.*

Water	1/4 cup	60 mL
Dry sherry	2 tbsp.	30 mL
Miso (see Note)	2 tbsp.	30 mL
Granulated sugar	1 tsp.	5 mL
Chili paste (sambal oelek)	1/2 tsp.	2 mL
Sesame oil	2 tsp.	10 mL
Grated carrot	3 tbsp.	50 mL
Green onions, sliced	2	2
Finely grated ginger root	1 tsp.	5 mL
Small garlic clove, minced	1	1
Water	2 1/2 cups	625 mL
Chicken stock	1 1/2 cups	375 mL
Shredded fresh spinach leaves, lightly packed	1/2 cup	125 mL
Firm tofu, cut into 1/2 inch (12 mm) pieces	3 oz.	85 g
Rice vermicelli, broken up, softened according to package directions (see Note)	1 1/2 oz.	43 g

Whisk first 5 ingredients in small bowl. Set aside.

Heat sesame oil in large saucepan on medium. Add next 4 ingredients.
Heat and stir for about 2 minutes until fragrant.

Add second amount of water and stock. Bring to a boil. Add miso mixture.
Reduce heat to medium. Boil gently, uncovered, for 2 minutes.

Add remaining 3 ingredients. Stir. Remove from heat. Let stand for about
3 minutes until spinach is wilted and tofu is heated through. Makes about
5 cups (1.25 L).

(continued on next page)

Brothy Bests

1 cup (250 mL): 107 Calories; 4.0 g Total Fat (1.2 g Mono, 1.9 g Poly, 0.7 g Sat); 0 mg Cholesterol; 13 g Carbohydrate; 1 g Fibre; 5 g Protein; 522 mg Sodium

Pictured on page 35.

Note: Miso is fermented soy bean paste. It is available in specialty Asian grocery stores.

Note: Rice vermicelli is a long, thin noodle made with rice flour. It can be found in the Asian section of your grocery store.

Tomato Shrimp Soup

An intriguing shrimp soup with tangy tomato, spicy chili and an exhilarating hint of orange. Add a bit more chili paste if you like lingering heat!

Cooking oil	1 tbsp.	15 mL
Chopped onion	1 cup	250 mL
Garlic cloves, minced (or 1/2 tsp., 2 mL, powder)	2	2
Chili paste (sambal oelek)	1/2 tsp.	2 mL
Can of diced tomatoes (with juice)	28 oz.	796 mL
Chicken stock	2 cups	500 mL
Sun-dried tomatoes in oil, blotted dry, chopped	1/4 cup	60 mL
Tomato paste (see Tip, page 49)	3 tbsp.	50 mL
Granulated sugar	1/2 tsp.	2 mL
Pepper	1/4 tsp.	1 mL
Fresh spinach leaves, lightly packed	2 cups	500 mL
Frozen uncooked shrimp (peeled and deveined), thawed and chopped	3/4 lb.	340 g
Grated orange zest	1 tsp.	5 mL

Heat cooking oil in large saucepan on medium. Add next 3 ingredients. Stir. Cook for 5 to 10 minutes, stirring often, until onion is softened.

Add next 6 ingredients. Stir. Bring to a boil. Reduce heat to medium-low. Simmer, covered, for 5 minutes to blend flavours.

Add remaining 3 ingredients. Heat and stir until shrimp turn pink and spinach is wilted. Makes about 7 1/2 cups (1.9 L).

1 cup (250 mL): 119 Calories; 3.7 g Total Fat (1.6 g Mono, 1.1 g Poly, 0.5 g Sat); 69 mg Cholesterol; 11 g Carbohydrate; 2 g Fibre; 12 g Protein; 500 mg Sodium

Curry Rice Soup

This soup will definitely curry your favour! Golden curry broth unites with the contrasting textures of crisp asparagus and soft rice—resulting in a feast for the senses. Adjust the amount of curry powder to your liking.

Cooking oil	2 tsp.	10 mL
Chopped onion	1 cup	250 mL
Chopped carrot	1 cup	250 mL
Chopped celery	1/2 cup	125 mL
Curry powder	1 – 3 tsp.	5 – 15 mL
Chicken (or vegetable) stock	4 cups	1 L
Water	2 cups	500 mL
Long grain white rice	1/4 cup	60 mL
Dry onion soup mix (stir before measuring)	2 tbsp.	30 mL
Chopped fresh asparagus	1 cup	250 mL

Heat cooking oil in large saucepan on medium. Add next 3 ingredients. Cook for 5 to 10 minutes, stirring often, until onion is softened.

Add curry powder. Heat and stir for about 1 minute until fragrant.

Add next 4 ingredients. Stir. Bring to a boil. Reduce heat to medium-low. Simmer, covered, for about 10 minutes until rice is almost tender.

Add asparagus. Simmer, covered, for about 3 minutes until asparagus is tender-crisp. Makes about 7 cups (1.75 L).

1 cup (250 mL): 83 Calories; 2.1 g Total Fat (1.0 g Mono, 0.5 g Poly, 0.5 g Sat); 0.2 mg Cholesterol; 14 g Carbohydrate; 2 g Fibre; 3 g Protein; 890 mg Sodium

1. Miso Soup With Noodles, page 32
2. Carrot Satay Soup, page 83
3. Hot And Sour Szechuan Soup, page 134

Props courtesy of: Cherison Enterprises Inc.
Canhome Global
Danesco Inc.

Brothy Bests

Cucumber Avocado Soup

It's easy being green with smooth, refreshing cucumber, citrus flavours and a burst of fresh basil. Add a slice of cucumber for the perfect garnish.

Ripe medium avocado	1	1
Chopped, peeled English cucumber	4 cups	1 L
Water	1 cup	250 mL
Plain yogurt	1 1/2 cups	375 mL
Extra virgin olive oil	3 tbsp.	50 mL
Lime juice	3 tbsp.	50 mL
Garlic clove, minced	1	1
Ground cumin	1/2 tsp.	2 mL
Salt	1 tsp.	5 mL
Pepper	1/4 tsp.	1 mL
Finely sliced green onion	2 tbsp.	30 mL
Finely shredded fresh basil	2 tbsp.	30 mL

Cut avocado in half. Remove pit. Scoop pulp into blender or food processor. Discard peel. Add cucumber and water. Process until smooth.

Add next 7 ingredients. Process until smooth. Transfer to large bowl.

Add green onion and basil. Stir. Chill, covered, for at least 2 hours until cold. Makes about 5 cups (1.25 L).

1 cup (250 mL): 203 Calories; 15.8 g Total Fat (10.3 g Mono, 1.6 g Poly, 2.9 g Sat); 5 mg Cholesterol; 12 g Carbohydrate; 2 g Fibre; 6 g Protein; 536 mg Sodium

Pictured at left.

1. Cucumber Avocado Soup, above
2. Summer Gazpacho, page 40
3. Butternut Apple Soup, page 38

Props courtesy of: Danesco Inc.
                      Pfaltzgraff Canada

Butternut Apple Soup

*The tastes of autumn unite—apple and roasted squash combine
in a delicate soup that is delicious served chilled or hot.
A garnish of toasted pecans adds a special touch.*

Cooking oil	1 tbsp.	15 mL
Chopped, peeled butternut squash	4 cups	1 L
Cooking oil	1 tbsp.	15 mL
Chopped, peeled cooking apple (such as McIntosh)	3 cups	750 mL
Chopped onion	1/2 cup	125 mL
Cans of condensed chicken broth (10 oz., 284 mL, each)	2	2
Water (see Note)	2 1/2 cups	625 mL
Ground cardamom	1/2 tsp.	2 mL
Chopped pecans, toasted (see Tip, page 83), for garnish		

Drizzle first amount of cooking oil over squash in large bowl. Stir until coated. Arrange in single layer on ungreased baking sheet with sides. Bake in 450°F (230°C) oven for about 20 minutes, stirring occasionally, until edges start to brown.

Heat second amount of cooking oil in large saucepan on medium-high. Add apple and onion. Cook for 5 to 10 minutes, stirring often, until onion is softened.

Add next 3 ingredients and squash. Stir. Bring to a boil. Reduce heat to medium. Simmer, covered, for about 15 minutes, stirring occasionally, until squash and apple are tender. Carefully process with hand blender or in blender until smooth (see Safety Tip). Transfer to large bowl. Cool at room temperature before covering. Chill for at least 2 hours until cold.

Garnish individual servings with pecans. Makes about 7 cups (1.75 L).

1 cup (250 mL): 133 Calories; 5.1 g Total Fat (2.8 g Mono, 1.5 g Poly, 0.6 g Sat); 1 mg Cholesterol; 19 g Carbohydrate; 2 g Fibre; 5 g Protein; 543 mg Sodium

Pictured on page 36.

Note: If preferred, substitute 5 cups (1.25 L) chicken stock for condensed chicken broth and water.

Safety Tip: Follow blender manufacturer's instructions for processing hot liquids.

Cucumber Gazpacho

*Smart Spaniards know the perfect way to cool down is to sup
on some fresh gazpacho. And even though the soup is served chilled,
you can always heat it up with a little extra jalapeño.*

White wine vinegar	1/4 cup	60 mL
Olive (or cooking) oil	1/4 cup	60 mL
Garlic cloves (or 1/2 tsp., 2 mL, powder)	2	2
Chopped, peeled English cucumber	9 cups	2.25 L
Chopped tomato	2 cups	500 mL
White bread slices, crusts removed	6	6
Green onions, sliced	8	8
Chopped fresh basil	1/4 cup	60 mL
Jalapeño pepper, halved, seeds and ribs removed (see Tip, page 26)	1	1
Salt	1/2 tsp.	2 mL
GARDEN TOPPING		
Diced English cucumber (with peel)	1/2 cup	125 mL
Diced tomato	1/2 cup	125 mL
Chopped green onion	2 tbsp.	30 mL
Chopped fresh basil	1 tbsp.	15 mL

Process first 3 ingredients in blender or food processor until smooth. Transfer to extra-large bowl.

Add next 7 ingredients. Stir well. Process in blender or food processor until smooth. Transfer to large bowl. Stir. Chill, covered, for at least 2 hours until cold. Makes about 8 cups (2 L).

Garden Topping: Combine all 4 ingredients in small bowl. Makes about 1 1/4 cups (300 mL) topping. Sprinkle on individual servings. Serves 6.

1 serving: 196 Calories; 11.0 g Total Fat (7.5 g Mono, 1.2 g Poly, 1.6 g Sat); trace Cholesterol; 22 g Carbohydrate; 3 g Fibre; 4 g Protein; 343 mg Sodium

Summer Gazpacho

Salsa fans will be shouting olé! The refreshing flavour of this chilled delight is perfectly balanced by the crunchy crouton garnish.

Baguette bread slices, 1 inch (2.5 cm) thick	2	2
Large tomatoes, peeled (see Tip, page 41), seeded and chopped	4	4
Chopped, peeled and seeded English cucumber	1 cup	250 mL
Chopped red pepper	1 cup	250 mL
Chopped red onion	1/2 cup	125 mL
Olive oil	2 1/2 tbsp.	37 mL
Red wine vinegar	2 1/2 tbsp.	37 mL
Garlic clove, minced	1	1
Lime juice	1 tbsp.	15 mL
Hot pepper sauce	1/2 tsp.	2 mL
Salt	1/2 tsp.	2 mL
Baguette bread slices, 1/2 inch (12 mm) thick	8	8
Olive oil	1 1/2 tsp.	7 mL

Put first amount of bread slices in small bowl. Pour water over top to cover. Soak for about 5 minutes until very soft. Drain. Squeeze water from bread.

Combine next 10 ingredients in large bowl. Process 3/4 cup (175 mL) tomato mixture in blender or food processor until finely chopped. Transfer to small bowl. Reserve and chill. Add wet bread to remaining tomato mixture. Process in blender or food processor until smooth. Chill, covered, for at least 2 hours until cold. Makes about 4 1/2 cups (1.1 L). Pour into 4 individual soup bowls.

Arrange second amount of bread slices on ungreased baking sheet. Brush with second amount of olive oil. Broil on top rack in oven for about 1 minute per side until golden. Place 2 slices on each soup. Spoon reserved tomato mixture over bread. Serves 4.

1 serving: 337 Calories; 13.1 g Total Fat (8.5 g Mono, 1.7 g Poly, 1.9 g Sat); 0 mg Cholesterol; 50 g Carbohydrate; 6 g Fibre; 8 g Protein; 716 mg Sodium

Pictured on page 36.

Vichyssoise

This chilled potato and leek soup is an international favourite. It's wonderful for a casual summer dinner or as an elegant addition to a fancier feast.

Butter (or hard margarine)	2 tsp.	10 mL
Sliced leek (white part only)	1 1/2 cups	375 mL
Chopped onion	1/2 cup	125 mL
Dried thyme	1/4 tsp.	1 mL
Chicken (or vegetable) stock	3 cups	750 mL
Chopped peeled potato	1 1/2 cups	375 mL
Bay leaf	1	1
Salt	1/4 tsp.	1 mL
Cayenne pepper	1/8 tsp.	0.5 mL
Half-and-half cream (or homogenized milk)	1/2 cup	125 mL

Chopped fresh chives, for garnish

Melt butter in large saucepan on medium. Add next 3 ingredients. Cook for 5 to 10 minutes, stirring often, until leek and onion are softened.

Add next 5 ingredients. Stir. Bring to a boil. Reduce heat to medium. Boil gently, uncovered, for 15 to 20 minutes, stirring occasionally, until potato is tender. Discard bay leaf. Carefully process with hand blender or in blender until smooth (see Safety Tip).

Add cream. Stir well. Transfer to large bowl. Cool at room temperature before covering. Chill for at least 2 hours until cold.

Garnish individual servings with chives. Makes about 5 cups (1.25 L).

1 cup (250 mL): 118 Calories; 4.6 g Total Fat (1.8 g Mono, 0.3 g Poly, 2.2 g Sat); 8 mg Cholesterol; 17 g Carbohydrate; 2 g Fibre; 3 g Protein; 672 mg Sodium

Safety Tip: Follow blender manufacturer's instructions for processing hot liquids.

 To peel tomatoes, cut an 'X' on the bottom of each tomato, just through the skin. Place tomatoes in boiling water for 30 seconds. Immediately transfer to a bowl of ice water. Let stand until cool enough to handle. Peel and discard skins.

Sweet Potato Vichyssoise

*This twist on the traditional vichyssoise forgoes regular potatoes
for sweet potatoes—giving it a unique flavour that's far from
ordinary. Our lime sour cream also adds a delicious tang.*

Butter (or hard margarine)	3 tbsp.	50 mL
Chopped, peeled sweet potato (or yam)	2 1/2 cups	625 mL
Sliced leek (white part only)	2 cups	500 mL
Chicken stock	4 cups	1 L
Chopped fresh thyme (or 1/2 tsp., 2 mL, dried)	2 tsp.	10 mL
Salt	1/2 tsp.	2 mL
Pepper	1/2 tsp.	2 mL
Whipping cream	1/2 cup	125 mL
LIME SOUR CREAM		
Sour cream	1/3 cup	75 mL
Lime juice	1 tbsp.	15 mL
Grated lime zest	1 tsp.	5 mL

Heat butter in large saucepan on medium until melted. Add sweet
potato and leek. Cook for about 5 minutes, stirring occasionally, until leek
is softened.

Add next 4 ingredients. Stir. Bring to a boil. Reduce heat to medium-low.
Simmer, partially covered, for about 20 minutes, stirring occasionally, until
sweet potato is tender.

Add whipping cream. Carefully process with hand blender or in blender until
smooth (see Safety Tip). Transfer to large bowl. Cool at room temperature
before covering. Chill for at least 2 hours until cold. Makes 6 cups (1.5 L).

Lime Sour Cream: Stir all 3 ingredients in small bowl. Makes about 1/3 cup
(75 mL) sour cream. Drizzle onto individual servings. Serves 6.

*1 serving: 228 Calories; 15.1 g Total Fat (4.2 g Mono, 0.6 g Poly, 9.4 g Sat); 45 mg Cholesterol;
21 g Carbohydrate; 3 g Fibre; 4 g Protein; 857 mg Sodium*

Safety Tip: Follow blender manufacturer's instructions for processing
hot liquids.

Melon Berry Soup

The colours in this vibrant soup excite the eye and the palate. Serve in chilled bowls for a light, refreshing dessert on a hot summer evening.

Chopped ripe cantaloupe	5 cups	1.25 L
White grape juice	1 cup	250 mL
Lemon juice	2 tbsp.	30 mL
Fresh (or frozen, thawed) raspberries	1 1/2 cups	375 mL
White grape juice	1/3 cup	75 mL

Process first 3 ingredients in blender or food processor until smooth. Transfer to medium bowl. Chill, covered, for at least 2 hours until cold. Makes about 4 1/2 cups (1.1 L).

Process raspberries and second amount of grape juice in blender or food processor until smooth. Strain through sieve into small bowl. Discard seeds. Chill, covered, for at least 2 hours until cold. Drizzle over individual servings. Serves 6.

1 serving: 96 Calories; 0.6 g Total Fat (trace Mono, 0.1 g Poly, trace Sat); 0 mg Cholesterol; 24 g Carbohydrate; 3 g Fibre; 2 g Protein; 13 mg Sodium

Pictured on page 107.

Paré Pointer
When robots eat uranium they get a-tomic ache.

Pineapple Mango Soup

*This sweet treat makes a perfect palate cleanser or
a refreshing dessert. Serve in punch cups for extra style points.*

Cans of sliced mango (with syrup), (14 oz., 398 mL, each)	2	2
Chopped fresh pineapple	6 cups	1.5 L
Coconut milk (or reconstituted from powder)	1/2 cup	125 mL

Process all 3 ingredients in blender or food processor until smooth. Press through sieve into large bowl. Discard solids. Stir. Chill, covered, for at least 2 hours until cold. Makes about 6 cups (1.5 L).

1 cup (250 mL): 237 Calories; 5.2 g Total Fat (0.3 g Mono, 0.3 g Poly, 3.9 g Sat); 0 mg Cholesterol; 52 g Carbohydrate; 3 g Fibre; 1 g Protein; 34 mg Sodium

Orange Cantaloupe Soup

*Charm the guests at your next outdoor dinner party with
this simple yet heavenly treat. Distinct orange, ginger and
vanilla flavours combine to cool down a hot summer.*

Chopped ripe cantaloupe	6 cups	1.5 L
Vanilla yogurt	1 cup	250 mL
Frozen concentrated orange juice, thawed	1/4 cup	60 mL
Minced crystallized ginger	2 tbsp.	30 mL

Process all 4 ingredients in blender or food processor until smooth. Transfer to large bowl. Chill, covered, for at least 2 hours until cold. Makes about 5 cups (1.25 L).

1 cup (250 mL): 153 Calories; 1.6 g Total Fat (0.3 g Mono, trace Poly, 0.6 g Sat); 3 mg Cholesterol; 33 g Carbohydrate; 2 g Fibre; 4 g Protein; 50 mg Sodium

Strawberry Rhubarb Soup

Never wonder what you're going to do with your bounty of garden rhubarb again! The sweet and sour flavours of strawberry and rhubarb mingle with citrusy orange to make a lovely fine-weather treat. Garnish each serving by pouring the whipping cream in a swirl. Accent with a small sprig of mint.

Water	2 cups	500 mL
Granulated sugar	3/4 cup	175 mL
Chopped frozen (or fresh) rhubarb	2 cups	500 mL
Chopped frozen (or fresh) strawberries	4 cups	1 L
Orange juice	1 1/4 cups	300 mL
Whipping cream (or half-and-half cream), for garnish		

Bring water and sugar to a boil in large saucepan, stirring occasionally. Add rhubarb. Reduce heat to medium. Boil gently, covered, for about 5 minutes until rhubarb is softened.

Add strawberries and orange juice. Stir. Cook for 2 to 3 minutes, stirring occasionally, until strawberries are softened. Remove from heat. Carefully process with hand blender or in blender until smooth. Transfer to medium bowl. Cool at room temperature before covering. Chill for at least 2 hours until cold.

Drizzle individual servings with whipping cream. Makes about 4 1/2 cups (1.1 L).

1 cup (250 mL): 256 Calories; 0.4 g Total Fat (0.1 g Mono, 0.1 g Poly, trace Sat); 0 mg Cholesterol; 65 g Carbohydrate; 5 g Fibre; 2 g Protein; 7 mg Sodium

---

Paré Pointer
When that person gets a brainstorm it's only a drizzle.

Easy Cioppino

Pronounced chuh-PEE-noh, *this very Italian sounding favourite actually hails from San Francisco. It's a fisherman's feast as well as a San Francisco treat! Using frozen mixed seafood for this stew eliminates the work of peeling shrimp and cleaning clams. Serve with crusty bread for dipping.*

Mussels	1 lb.	454 g
Olive (or cooking) oil	3 tbsp.	50 mL
Garlic cloves, minced	2	2
Diced green pepper	3/4 cup	175 mL
Diced onion	3/4 cup	175 mL
Diced celery	1/4 cup	60 mL
Bay leaf	1	1
Dried oregano	1/2 tsp.	2 mL
Salt	1/2 tsp.	2 mL
Pepper	1/4 tsp.	1 mL
Fennel seed	1/4 tsp.	1 mL
Dry (or alcohol-free) white wine	3/4 cup	175 mL
Worcestershire sauce	1 tbsp.	15 mL
Clam tomato beverage (or clam juice or fish stock), see Note	2 cups	500 mL
Can of diced tomatoes (with juice)	14 oz.	398 mL
Water	1/2 cup	125 mL
Granulated sugar	2 tsp.	10 mL
Package of frozen mixed seafood, thawed	12 oz.	340 g
Cod fillets (or other white fish), any small bones removed, cut into 1 inch (2.5 cm) pieces	1/2 lb.	225 g
Lemon juice	1 tbsp.	15 mL
Chopped fresh basil	2 tbsp.	30 mL
Chopped fresh parsley	2 tbsp.	30 mL

Put mussels into medium bowl. Lightly tap any that are opened 1/4 inch (6 mm) or more. Discard any that do not close. Set aside.

(continued on next page)

Put olive oil and garlic into large saucepan. Cook on medium for 2 to 3 minutes, stirring often, until fragrant.

Add next 8 ingredients. Stir. Cook for about 5 minutes, stirring occasionally, until vegetables start to soften.

Add wine and Worcestershire sauce. Bring to a boil. Cook, uncovered, for about 5 minutes until liquid is reduced by half.

Add next 4 ingredients. Bring to a boil.

Add next 3 ingredients and mussels. Reduce heat to medium. Boil gently, covered, for about 4 minutes until mussels are opened and fish flakes easily when tested with fork. Discard bay leaf and any unopened mussels.

Add basil and parsley. Stir. Makes about 9 cups (2.25 L).

1 cup (250 mL): 188 Calories; 6.2 g Total Fat (3.6 g Mono, 0.9 g Poly, 0.9 g Sat); 62 mg Cholesterol; 14 g Carbohydrate; 1 g Fibre; 16 g Protein; 602 mg Sodium

Pictured on page 54.

Note: Using clam tomato beverage will result in a stronger tomato flavour than using clam juice or fish stock.

Paré Pointer
Some students should consider joining the submarine section of the navy—if their marks are below C level.

Pasta e Fagioli

While you're out on the gondola, consider romancing
your slow cooker with this Italian favourite.

Bacon slices, diced	6	6
Chopped onion	1 cup	250 mL
Sliced celery	1 cup	250 mL
Sliced carrot	1 cup	250 mL
Dried oregano	1 tsp.	5 mL
Dried basil	1 tsp.	5 mL
Garlic cloves, minced (or 1/2 tsp., 2 mL, powder)	2	2
Pepper	1/2 tsp.	2 mL
Can of white kidney beans, rinsed and drained	19 oz.	540 mL
Can of diced tomatoes (with juice)	28 oz.	796 mL
Chicken stock	3 cups	750 mL
Water	1 cup	250 mL
Tomato paste (see Tip, page 49)	1/4 cup	60 mL
Bay leaves	2	2
Tubetti (or other very small pasta)	1 cup	250 mL
Chopped fresh parsley	2 tbsp.	30 mL
Grated Parmesan cheese	1/4 cup	60 mL

Cook bacon in medium frying pan on medium until crisp. Transfer to 4 to 5 quart (4 to 5 L) slow cooker using slotted spoon.

Heat 2 tsp. (10 mL) drippings in same frying pan on medium. Add next 7 ingredients. Cook for 5 to 10 minutes, stirring often, until onion is softened. Add to slow cooker.

Measure 1 cup (250 mL) kidney beans onto plate. Mash with fork. Add to slow cooker. Add remaining kidney beans to slow cooker.

Add next 5 ingredients. Stir. Cook, covered, on Low for 7 to 8 hours or on High for 3 1/2 to 4 hours until vegetables are tender. Discard bay leaves.

(continued on next page)

Cook pasta in boiling salted water in large uncovered saucepan for 10 to 12 minutes, stirring occasionally, until tender but firm. Drain. Add to slow cooker.

Add parsley. Stir.

Sprinkle Parmesan cheese on individual servings. Makes about 12 cups (3 L).

1 cup (250 mL): 145 Calories; 3.7 g Total Fat (1.3 g Mono, 0.5 g Poly, 1.5 g Sat); 5 mg Cholesterol; 22 g Carbohydrate; 2 g Fibre; 7 g Protein; 440 mg Sodium

Pictured on page 126.

 If a recipe calls for less than an entire can of tomato paste, freeze the unopened can for 30 minutes. Open both ends and push the contents through one end. Slice off only what you need. Freeze the remaining paste in a resealable freezer bag or plastic wrap for future use.

Shrimp Bisque

Traditionally, bisque, a rich velvety seafood soup, is served only at fine dining establishments. We've made this recipe easy enough for you to serve at your fine dining room table. It's an excellent starter for a special dinner party. Like the bones in a meat stock, the shrimp shells are used to add flavour.

Bag of frozen uncooked shrimp (shell-on and deveined), thawed (see Note)	1 lb.	454 g
Cooking oil	1 tsp.	5 mL
Chopped onion	1 cup	250 mL
Chopped carrot	1/2 cup	125 mL
Chopped celery	1/2 cup	125 mL
Garlic clove, chopped (or 1/4 tsp., 1 mL, powder)	1	1
Tomato paste (see Tip, page 49)	1 tbsp.	15 mL
Dry (or alcohol-free) white wine	1 cup	250 mL
Water	5 cups	1.25 L
Whole black peppercorns	8	8
Bay leaf	1	1
Butter (or hard margarine)	1/4 cup	60 mL
All-purpose flour	1/4 cup	60 mL
Whipping cream	1/2 cup	125 mL
Brandy (optional)	2 tbsp.	30 mL
Salt	1/4 tsp.	1 mL

Chopped fresh dill, for garnish

Peel shrimp, reserving shells. Chop shrimp. Chill.

Heat cooking oil in large saucepan on medium. Add reserved shrimp shells and next 4 ingredients. Cook for about 10 minutes, stirring occasionally, until vegetables start to brown.

Add tomato paste. Mix well. Add wine, stirring constantly and scraping any brown bits from bottom of pan, until boiling.

(continued on next page)

Bistro Favourites

Add next 3 ingredients. Bring to a boil. Reduce heat to medium-low. Simmer, partially covered, for about 15 minutes, stirring occasionally, until vegetables are soft. Strain through sieve into medium bowl. Discard solids.

Melt butter in same large saucepan on medium. Add flour. Stir constantly until mixture comes together to make roux (see Thickening Tricks, page 9). Slowly add 2 cups (500 mL) strained liquid, stirring constantly with whisk until boiling and thickened. Add shrimp and remaining strained liquid. Cook for about 5 minutes, stirring often, until shrimp turn pink.

Add next 3 ingredients. Heat and stir for 2 to 3 minutes until heated through.

Garnish individual servings with dill. Makes 6 cups (1.5 L).

1 cup (250 mL): 263 Calories; 16.8 g Total Fat (4.9 g Mono, 1.2 g Poly, 9.6 g Sat); 133 mg Cholesterol; 9 g Carbohydrate; 1 g Fibre; 13 g Protein; 287 mg Sodium

Pictured on page 89.

Note: If you purchase shrimp that is not already deveined, remove and reserve shells. Use a small, sharp knife to make a shallow cut along the centre of back. Rinse under cold water to wash out the dark vein.

Paré Pointer
The sun and bread—one rises from the East
and the other from the yeast.

Scotch Broth

If you prefer, substitute beef for lamb in this slow cooker soup.

Cooking oil	1 tbsp.	15 mL
Stewing lamb (or beef), cut into 1/2 inch (12 mm) pieces	1 1/2 lbs.	680 g
Chopped onion	2 cups	500 mL
Chopped carrot	1 1/2 cups	375 mL
Chopped yellow turnip	1 cup	250 mL
Pearl barley	2/3 cup	150 mL
Chopped celery	1/2 cup	125 mL
Beef stock	8 cups	2 L
Salt	1/2 tsp.	2 mL
Pepper	1/4 tsp.	1 mL
Frozen peas	1/2 cup	125 mL
Chopped fresh parsley (or 1 tbsp., 15 mL, flakes)	1/4 cup	60 mL

Heat cooking oil in large frying pan on medium-high. Add lamb. Cook for 8 to 10 minutes, stirring occasionally, until browned. Transfer to 4 to 5 quart (4 to 5 L) slow cooker.

Add next 8 ingredients. Stir. Cook, covered, on Low for 8 to 10 hours or on High for 4 to 5 hours until lamb and barley are tender.

Add peas and parsley. Stir. Cook, covered, on High for about 5 minutes until peas are tender. Makes about 12 cups (3 L).

1 cup (250 mL): 168 Calories; 4.4 g Total Fat (1.9 g Mono, 0.7 g Poly, 1.2 g Sat); 37 mg Cholesterol; 16 g Carbohydrate; 3 g Fibre; 16 g Protein; 733 mg Sodium

Pictured at right.

1. Scotch Broth, above
2. French Onion Soup, page 61
3. Mulligatawny Soup, page 60

Props courtesy of: Pfaltzgraff Canada
Winners Stores

Green Pea Soup

*This savoury ham and green pea soup is as thick
as...well...pea soup! Comforting, satisfying and filling.*

Water	7 cups	1.75 L
Green split peas, rinsed and drained	1 1/2 cups	375 mL
Chopped onion	1 cup	250 mL
Chopped carrot	1/2 cup	125 mL
Chopped celery	1/2 cup	125 mL
Chicken bouillon powder	2 tsp.	10 mL
Garlic clove, minced (or 1/4 tsp., 1 mL, powder)	1	1
Bay leaf	1	1
Pepper	1/4 tsp.	1 mL
Diced cooked ham	2 cups	500 mL

Put first 9 ingredients into large saucepan. Stir. Bring to a boil. Reduce
heat to medium-low. Simmer, covered, for about 1 1/2 hours, stirring
occasionally, until split peas are very soft. Discard bay leaf. Carefully process
with hand blender or in blender until smooth (see Safety Tip).

Add ham. Stir. Cook for about 5 minutes, stirring occasionally, until heated
through. Makes about 7 cups (1.75 L).

*1 cup (250 mL): 247 Calories; 4.6 g Total Fat (2.1 g Mono, 0.9 g Poly, 1.4 g Sat); 25 mg Cholesterol;
31 g Carbohydrate; 4 g Fibre; 21 g Protein; 843 mg Sodium*

Safety Tip: Follow blender manufacturer's instructions for processing
hot liquids.

1. Catch Of The Day Chowder, page 67
2. Easy Cioppino, page 46

Props courtesy of: Danesco Inc.
                     Pier 1 Imports

Italian Wedding Soup

Meatballs and pasta in a soup—a happy union, indeed!

Large egg	1	1
Grated Romano (or Parmesan) cheese	1/4 cup	60 mL
Fine dry bread crumbs	1/4 cup	60 mL
Milk	1/4 cup	60 mL
Garlic clove, minced (or 1/4 tsp., 1 mL, powder)	1	1
Pepper	1/4 tsp.	1 mL
Ground nutmeg	1/8 tsp.	0.5 mL
Lean ground beef	1/2 lb.	225 g
Olive (or cooking) oil	1 tbsp.	15 mL
Diced onion	1/2 cup	125 mL
Diced carrot	1/2 cup	125 mL
Diced celery	1/2 cup	125 mL
Chicken stock	6 cups	1.5 L
Finely chopped fresh parsley (or 1 tbsp., 15 mL, flakes)	1/4 cup	60 mL
Dried oregano	1/2 tsp.	2 mL
Pepper	1/4 tsp.	1 mL
Acini del pepe (or other very small) pasta	1/2 cup	125 mL
Chopped fresh spinach leaves, lightly packed	3 cups	750 mL
Grated Romano (or Parmesan) cheese	1/4 cup	60 mL

Combine first 7 ingredients in medium bowl.

Add beef. Mix well. Roll into 1/2 inch (12 mm) balls. Arrange on greased baking sheet with sides. Bake in 350°F (175°C) oven for 10 minutes. Transfer to paper towels to drain. Makes about 95 meatballs. Set aside.

Heat olive oil in large saucepan on medium. Add next 3 ingredients. Cook for 5 to 10 minutes, stirring often, until onion is softened.

Add next 4 ingredients. Bring to a boil.

Add pasta and meatballs. Stir. Cook, partially covered, for 10 to 12 minutes, stirring occasionally, until pasta is tender but firm.

(continued on next page)

Add spinach and cheese. Heat and stir for 1 to 2 minutes until spinach is wilted and cheese is melted. Makes about 8 cups (2 L).

1 cup (250 mL): 183 Calories; 9.3 g Total Fat (4.0 g Mono, 0.6 g Poly, 3.8 g Sat); 50 mg Cholesterol; 13 g Carbohydrate; 2 g Fibre; 12 g Protein; 818 mg Sodium

---

Vegetarian Borscht

Velvety vegetable purée with chunks of dark red beets. In keeping with Russian and Polish tradition, serve this soup with a dollop of sour cream.

Butter (or hard margarine)	1 tbsp.	15 mL
Chopped brown (or white) mushrooms	1 1/2 cups	375 mL
Chopped onion	1 cup	250 mL
All-purpose flour	2 tsp.	10 mL
Vegetable stock	6 cups	1.5 L
Medium beets, peeled and cut into 1/2 inch (12 mm) pieces (see Tip, page 22)	3	3
Grated carrot	1/2 cup	125 mL
Tomato paste (see Tip, page 49)	2 tbsp.	30 mL
Granulated sugar	1/2 tsp.	2 mL
Pepper	1/4 tsp.	1 mL
Lemon juice	2 tbsp.	30 mL
Sour cream (optional)	1/3 cup	75 mL

Melt butter in large saucepan on medium-high. Add mushrooms and onion. Cook for 5 to 10 minutes, stirring occasionally, until onion is softened and mushroom liquid is evaporated.

Sprinkle with flour. Heat and stir for 1 minute.

Add next 6 ingredients. Stir. Bring to a boil. Reduce heat to medium-low. Simmer, partially covered, for about 45 minutes, stirring occasionally, until beets are very tender. Remove from heat.

Add lemon juice. Stir. Carefully transfer about 2 cups (500 mL) vegetables to blender or food processor with slotted spoon. Process until smooth (see Safety Tip). Return to saucepan. Stir.

Add sour cream. Heat on medium for about 2 minutes, stirring with whisk, until heated through. Makes about 8 cups (2 L).

1 cup (250 mL): 66 Calories; 2.0 g Total Fat (0.5 g Mono, 0.1 g Poly, 1.3 g Sat); 4 mg Cholesterol; 10 g Carbohydrate; 2 g Fibre; 3 g Protein; 699 mg Sodium

Safety Tip: Follow manufacturer's instructions for processing hot liquids.

Cock-A-Leekie

You needn't search the Scottish moors for a taste of its traditional fare. Sound the bagpipes, this soup comes straight from the Highlands to your slow cooker. And although the name seems a bit nonsensical, it's actually derived from its traditional ingredients: cock, for rooster; and leekie, for leeks.

Bacon slices, diced	4	4
Sliced leek (white part only)	4 cups	1 L
Salt	1/2 tsp.	2 mL
Pearl barley	1/2 cup	125 mL
Chopped carrot	1 cup	250 mL
Chopped celery	1/2 cup	125 mL
Bone-in chicken parts, skin removed (see Note)	3 1/2 lb.	1.6 kg
Chicken stock	7 cups	1.75 L
PEPPER BOUQUET GARNI		
Whole black peppercorns	8	8
Fresh parsley sprigs	4	4
Fresh thyme sprig	1	1
Bay leaf	1	1
Can of evaporated milk	3 3/4 oz.	110 mL
All-purpose flour	1 tbsp.	15 mL

Cook bacon in large frying pan on medium for about 5 minutes until almost crisp.

Add leek. Sprinkle with salt. Cook, stirring occasionally, for about 5 minutes until leek starts to soften. Transfer to 5 to 7 quart (5 to 7 L) slow cooker.

Layer next 4 ingredients, in order given, over leek mixture. Add stock.

Pepper Bouquet Garni: Place first 4 ingredients on 10 inch (25 cm) square piece of cheesecloth. Draw up corners and tie with butcher's string. Submerge in liquid in slow cooker. Cook, covered, on Low for 8 to 10 hours or on High for 4 to 5 hours. Remove and discard bouquet garni. Remove chicken to cutting board using slotted spoon. Remove chicken from bones. Discard bones. Chop chicken into bite-size pieces. Return to slow cooker.

(continued on next page)

Stir evaporated milk into flour with whisk in small bowl until smooth. Add to soup. Stir well. Cook, covered, on High for about 5 minutes until boiling and slightly thickened. Makes about 12 cups (3 L).

1 cup (250 mL): 270 Calories; 8.5 g Total Fat (3.9 g Mono, 2.0 g Poly, 3.3 g Sat); 98 mg Cholesterol; 15 g Carbohydrate; 2 g Fibre; 32 g Protein; 1141 mg Sodium

Note: Use whichever cuts of chicken you prefer as long as the weight used is equal to that listed.

Paré Pointer

First Man: *Tell me who is a big tough guy and I'll tell you who is a fraidy-cat coward.*

Second Man: *I'm a big tough guy.*

First Man: *I'm a fraidy-cat coward!*

Mulligatawny Soup

Mulligatawny can literally be translated as "pepper water." But that is hardly a fitting description for our version of this classic soup—a magnificent blend of curry, chicken, coconut and apple, without even a dash of pepper!

Cooking oil	1 tbsp.	15 mL
Chopped onion	1 1/2 cups	375 mL
Sliced celery	3/4 cup	175 mL
Sliced carrot	3/4 cup	175 mL
Garlic cloves, minced (or 1/2 tsp., 2 mL, powder)	2	2
Finely grated ginger root	2 tsp.	10 mL
Curry powder	1 tbsp.	15 mL
Chicken stock	4 cups	1 L
Diced, peeled tart apple (such as Granny Smith)	1 1/4 cups	300 mL
Chopped peeled potato	1 cup	250 mL
Can of coconut milk	14 oz.	398 mL
Chopped cooked chicken	1 cup	250 mL
Sweetened applesauce	1/2 cup	125 mL
Salt	1/4 tsp.	1 mL

Heat cooking oil in large saucepan on medium. Add next 5 ingredients. Cook for about 5 to 10 minutes, stirring often, until onion is softened.

Add curry powder. Heat and stir for about 1 minute until vegetables are coated and curry is fragrant.

Add next 3 ingredients. Stir. Bring to a boil. Reduce heat to medium-low. Simmer, covered, for about 20 minutes, stirring occasionally, until potato is tender.

Add remaining 4 ingredients. Stir. Cook for about 5 minutes until heated through. Makes about 9 cups (2.25 L).

1 cup (250 mL): 203 Calories; 12.7 g Total Fat (1.9 g Mono, 1.0 g Poly, 8.8 g Sat); 19.6 mg Cholesterol; 15 g Carbohydrate; 2 g Fibre; 9 g Protein; 493 mg Sodium

Pictured on page 53.

French Onion Soup

Mais oui, a chic Parisian would never dream of spending hours slaving over a hot stove, so why should you? Just let your slow cooker do the work for you.

Thinly sliced onion	5 cups	1.25 L
Butter (or hard margarine), melted	2 tbsp.	30 mL
Olive (or cooking) oil	2 tbsp.	30 mL
Dried thyme	1/2 tsp.	2 mL
Beef stock	8 cups	2 L
Medium sherry	1/4 cup	60 mL
Salt, just a pinch (optional)		
Baguette bread slices, about 1/2 inch (12 mm) thick	12	12
Grated Gruyére (or mozzarella) cheese	3/4 cup	175 mL

Put onion into 3 1/2 to 4 quart (3.5 to 4 L) slow cooker. Add butter and olive oil. Stir until coated. Sprinkle with thyme. Cook, covered, on High for about 6 hours until onion is caramelized.

Heat stock in large saucepan on medium until almost boiling. Add sherry and salt. Stir. Carefully add to slow cooker. Stir. Cook, covered, on High for 20 minutes to blend flavours. Makes about 10 cups (2.5 L).

Place bread slices on ungreased baking sheet. Broil on centre rack for about 3 minutes until golden. Turn slices. Sprinkle with cheese. Broil for about 3 minutes until cheese is melted and golden. Divide soup among 6 bowls. Top each with 2 cheese toasts. Serve immediately. Serves 6.

1 serving: 285 Calories; 14.1 g Total Fat (6.3 g Mono, 1.0 g Poly, 5.9 g Sat); 26 mg Cholesterol; 25 g Carbohydrate; 3 g Fibre; 12 g Protein; 1367 mg Sodium

Pictured on page 53.

BAKED FRENCH ONION SOUP: Broil bread slices on one side only. Divide soup among 6 ovenproof bowls. Place 2 bread slices in each bowl, toasted side down. Sprinkle about 3 tbsp. (50 mL) grated Gruyére (or mozzarella) cheese in each bowl. Broil for about 5 minutes until cheese is melted and golden. Serve immediately. Bowls will be very hot!

Won Ton Soup

Are you wantin' some won ton? The shrimp-filled dumplings in this delicious ginger and onion broth serve as a unique variation of the everyday won ton soup.

Frozen uncooked shrimp (peeled and deveined), thawed	1/2 lb.	225 g
Chopped green onion	1/4 cup	60 mL
Soy sauce	2 tsp.	10 mL
Cornstarch	2 tsp.	10 mL
Garlic clove, minced (or 1/4 tsp., 1 mL, powder)	1	1
Finely grated ginger root	1 tsp.	5 mL
Sesame oil (optional)	1 tsp.	5 mL
Water	1/4 cup	60 mL
Cornstarch	1 tbsp.	15 mL
Round dumpling wrappers, thawed	48	48
Chicken stock	6 cups	1.5 L
Water	1 cup	250 mL
Dry sherry	1 tbsp.	15 mL
Sesame oil (optional)	1 tsp.	5 mL
Piece of gingerroot (1/2 inch, 12 mm, length)	1	1
Sliced suey choy (Chinese cabbage)	1 cup	250 mL
Sliced fresh white mushrooms	1/2 cup	125 mL
Chopped green onion	1/4 cup	60 mL

Put first 7 ingredients into food processor. Process with on/off motion until shrimp is finely chopped. Set aside.

Stir water into second amount of cornstarch in small bowl until smooth.

Place 8 wrappers on work surface. Cover remaining wrappers with damp towel to prevent drying. Place about 1 tsp. (5 mL) shrimp mixture slightly off-centre on one side of each wrapper. Dampen edges of wrappers with cornstarch mixture. Fold in half over filling. Crimp edges to seal. Cover filled won tons with damp towel to prevent drying. Repeat, in batches, with remaining wrappers and filling.

(continued on next page)

Bistro Favourites

Put next 5 ingredients into large saucepan. Bring to a boil. Add won tons. Return to a boil. Reduce heat to medium. Boil gently, uncovered, for 5 minutes.

Add remaining 3 ingredients. Cook for about 3 minutes until won tons are tender and filling is pink. Discard gingerroot. Makes about 9 cups (2.25 L).

1 cup (250 mL): 183 Calories; 2.5 g Total Fat (0.6 g Mono, 0.9 g Poly, 0.7 g Sat); 42 mg Cholesterol; 29 g Carbohydrate; 1 g Fibre; 11 g Protein; 933 mg Sodium

Variation: Traditional won ton soup uses ground pork instead of shrimp. Substitute 1/2 lb. (225 g) ground pork for shrimp. Cook as directed.

Paré Pointer
"I just swallowed a bone."
"Are you choking?"
"No, I'm serious."

Roasted Vegetable Chowder

Be daringly decadent when dining on this delight. The sweet roasted
vegetables in a creamy broth will have you asking for seconds.

Olive (or cooking) oil	3 tbsp.	50 mL
Dried rosemary, crushed	1 tsp.	5 mL
Garlic powder	1/2 tsp.	2 mL
Salt	1/4 tsp.	1 mL
Pepper	1/4 tsp.	1 mL
Asian eggplant (with peel), quartered lengthwise and cut into 1/2 inch (12 mm) pieces	1	1
Small zucchini (with peel), quartered lengthwise and cut into 1/2 inch (12 mm) pieces	1	1
Fresh whole white mushrooms, quartered	2 cups	500 mL
Diced unpeeled potato	2 cups	500 mL
Chopped onion	1 cup	250 mL
Diced red pepper	1 cup	250 mL
Diced green pepper	1 cup	250 mL
Vegetable (or chicken) stock	6 cups	1.5 L
Chopped fresh thyme	1 tbsp.	15 mL
Whipping cream	1/2 cup	125 mL
Cornstarch	2 tbsp.	30 mL

Combine first 5 ingredients in large bowl.

Add next 7 ingredients. Stir until coated. Arrange vegetables in single layer on ungreased baking sheet with sides. Bake in 450°F (230°C) oven for 30 to 45 minutes, stirring occasionally, until vegetables are tender.

Bring stock to a boil in large saucepan. Add thyme and roasted vegetables. Stir. Simmer, partially covered, on medium-low for 10 minutes to blend flavours.

Stir cream into cornstarch in small cup. Slowly stir into soup. Heat and stir until boiling and thickened. Makes about 9 1/2 cups (2.4 L).

1 cup (250 mL): 147 Calories; 9.2 g Total Fat (4.5 g Mono, 0.6 g Poly, 3.6 g Sat); 15 mg Cholesterol; 15 g Carbohydrate; 2 g Fibre; 3 g Protein; 615 mg Sodium

Pictured on page 71.

Smoked Cod And Clam Chowder

Avast, ye mateys! The smoky fish flavour of this creamy
clam chowder will have seafood lovers dropping anchor.

Butter (or hard margarine)	1 tbsp.	15 mL
Chopped onion	1 1/2 cups	375 mL
All-purpose flour	2 tbsp.	30 mL
Chopped peeled potato	3 cups	750 mL
Water	3 cups	750 mL
Bay leaf	1	1
Salt	1/2 tsp.	2 mL
Pepper	1/4 tsp.	1 mL
Can of whole baby clams	5 oz.	142 g
Smoked cod fillet	12 oz.	340 g
Can of evaporated milk	13 1/2 oz.	385 mL
Chopped fresh parsley (or 1 tsp., 5 mL, flakes)	3 tbsp.	50 mL
Lemon juice	2 tbsp.	30 mL

Melt butter in large saucepan on medium. Add onion. Cook for 5 to 10 minutes, stirring often, until softened.

Sprinkle with flour. Heat and stir for 1 minute.

Add next 5 ingredients. Heat and stir until boiling and thickened.

Drain clam liquid into same saucepan, reserving clams. Stir. Add cod to soup. Bring to a boil. Reduce heat to medium-low. Simmer, partially covered, for 15 to 20 minutes, stirring occasionally, until potato is tender. Remove from heat. Discard bay leaf. Remove cod to cutting board with slotted spoon. Cut into 1/2 inch (12 mm) pieces. Remove 1 cup (250 mL) potato mixture with slotted spoon to small bowl. Carefully process remaining potato mixture with hand blender or in blender until smooth (see Safety Tip).

Add evaporated milk, reserved clams, cod and potato mixture. Heat and stir for about 5 minutes until heated through.

Add parsley and lemon juice. Stir. Makes about 9 cups (2.25 L).

1 cup (250 mL): 190 Calories; 5.6 g Total Fat (1.5 g Mono, 0.3 g Poly, 3.0 g Sat); 28 mg Cholesterol; 19 g Carbohydrate; 1 g Fibre; 16 g Protein; 565 mg Sodium

Safety Tip: Follow manufacturer's instructions for processing hot liquids.

Chili Corn Chowder

This corn chowder has been given some zip with jalapeño, salsa and chili powder. Serve with crisp tortilla chips for a crunchy dipper.

Bacon slices, diced	4	4
Chopped onion	1 cup	250 mL
Chopped celery	1 cup	250 mL
Jalapeño pepper, seeds and ribs removed, finely diced (see Tip, page 26)	1	1
Diced unpeeled red potato	2 cups	500 mL
Frozen kernel corn	2 cups	500 mL
Chicken stock	1 1/2 cups	375 mL
Can of cream-style corn	10 oz.	284 mL
Chili powder	1 tsp.	5 mL
Ground cumin	1/2 tsp.	2 mL
Salt	1/2 tsp.	2 mL
Milk	1 cup	250 mL
Medium salsa	1/4 cup	60 mL
Chopped fresh basil	2 tbsp.	30 mL

Cook bacon in large saucepan on medium until crisp. Drain all but 2 tsp. (10 mL) of drippings.

Add next 3 ingredients. Cook for 5 to 10 minutes, stirring often, until onion is softened.

Add next 7 ingredients. Bring to a boil. Reduce heat to medium-low. Simmer, partially covered, for 15 to 20 minutes, stirring occasionally, until potato is tender.

Add remaining 3 ingredients. Heat and stir for about 5 minutes until heated through. Makes about 6 1/2 cups (1.6 L).

1 cup (250 mL): 170 Calories; 4.5 g Total Fat (1.8 g Mono, 0.7 g Poly, 1.7 g Sat); 6 mg Cholesterol; 29 g Carbohydrate; 3 g Fibre; 7 g Protein; 565 mg Sodium

Variation: Omit basil. Add 2 tbsp. (30 mL) chopped fresh cilantro.

Catch Of The Day Chowder

The best buccaneers know that smoky bacon is the perfect complement in this stew-like tomato soup. Garnish with fresh thyme for the perfect touch.

Bacon slices, diced	4	4
Chopped onion	1 cup	250 mL
Diced peeled potato	2 cups	500 mL
Cans of diced tomatoes (with juice), (14 oz., 398 mL, each)	2	2
Can of tomato sauce	14 oz.	398 mL
Soy sauce	3 tbsp.	50 mL
Garlic powder	1/2 tsp.	2 mL
Dried thyme	1/2 tsp.	2 mL
Pepper	1/2 tsp.	2 mL
Snapper fillets (or other white fish), any small bones removed, cut into 1 inch (2.5 cm) pieces	1/2 lb.	225 g
Milk	1 cup	250 mL

Cook bacon in large saucepan on medium until crisp. Drain all but 2 tsp. (10 mL) drippings.

Add onion. Cook for 5 to 10 minutes, stirring often, until onion is softened.

Add next 7 ingredients. Bring to a boil. Reduce heat to medium-low. Simmer, covered, for about 25 minutes, stirring occasionally, until potato is tender.

Add snapper and milk. Stir. Cook, covered, for 8 to 10 minutes until fish flakes easily when tested with fork. Makes about 8 1/2 cups (2.1 L).

1 cup (250 mL): 141 Calories; 3.6 g Total Fat (1.4 g Mono, 0.6 g Poly, 1.3 g Sat); 15 mg Cholesterol; 18 g Carbohydrate; 2 g Fibre; 10 g Protein; 899 mg Sodium

Pictured on page 54.

Two Potato Chowder

One potato, two potato—tastes like you need a spoonful more! Smoky bacon and rustic potatoes combine in this comforting, old-fashioned chowder.

Bacon slices, diced	6	6
Chopped onion	1 cup	250 mL
Diced celery	1 cup	250 mL
All-purpose flour	2 tbsp.	30 mL
Chicken stock	4 cups	1 L
Diced, peeled sweet potato (or yam)	1 1/2 cups	375 mL
Diced unpeeled red potato	1 1/2 cups	375 mL
Dried rosemary, crushed	1/4 tsp.	1 mL
Ground thyme	1/4 tsp.	1 mL
Pepper	1/4 tsp.	1 mL
Milk	1 cup	250 mL

Cook bacon in large saucepan on medium until almost crisp. Drain all but 2 tsp. (10 mL) drippings. Add onion and celery. Cook for 5 to 10 minutes, stirring often, until onion is softened.

Sprinkle with flour. Heat and stir for 1 minute.

Slowly add 1 cup (250 mL) stock. Heat and stir until boiling and thickened. Add remaining stock. Stir. Bring to a boil.

Add next 5 ingredients. Stir. Reduce heat to medium-low. Simmer, partially covered, for 15 to 20 minutes, stirring occasionally, until potato is tender.

Add milk. Heat and stir for 1 to 2 minutes until heated through. Makes about 8 cups (2 L).

1 cup (250 mL): 127 Calories; 4.2 g Total Fat (1.7 g Mono, 0.5 g Poly, 1.8 g Sat); 6 mg Cholesterol; 18 g Carbohydrate; 2 g Fibre; 5 g Protein; 541 mg Sodium

Ham And Cheese Chowder

The tastes of ham and cheese in a soup, please! This kid-friendly chowder is simple to prepare and has a quick cooking time. Perfect for lunch.

Butter (or hard margarine)	2 tbsp.	30 mL
Chopped onion	1 cup	250 mL
All-purpose flour	2 tbsp.	30 mL
Dill weed	1/2 tsp.	2 mL
Pepper	1/4 tsp.	1 mL
Chicken stock	2 cups	500 mL
Diced peeled potato	2 cups	500 mL
Grated medium Cheddar cheese	2 cups	500 mL
Milk	1 cup	250 mL
Diced cooked ham	1 cup	250 mL

Melt butter in large saucepan on medium. Add onion. Cook for 5 to 10 minutes, stirring often, until softened.

Add next 3 ingredients. Heat and stir for 1 minute.

Slowly stir in stock until combined. Heat and stir until boiling.

Add potato. Stir. Bring to a boil. Reduce heat to medium-low. Simmer, partially covered, for 15 to 20 minutes, stirring occasionally, until potato is tender.

Add remaining 3 ingredients. Heat and stir for about 5 minutes until heated through. Makes about 5 cups (1.25 L).

1 cup (250 mL): 390 Calories; 24.1 g Total Fat (7.3 g Mono, 1.1 g Poly, 14.5 g Sat); 82 mg Cholesterol; 21 g Carbohydrate; 2 g Fibre; 23 g Protein; 1165 mg Sodium

Manhattan Clam Chowder

*No need to man the helm—your slow cooker will take over in
our version of this traditional tomato-based clam chowder.
Serve with buns or crusty bread for dunking.*

Cans of whole baby clams (5 oz., 142 g, each)	2	2
Water	6 cups	1.5 L
Cans of diced tomatoes (with juice), (14 oz., 398 mL, each)	2	2
Chopped unpeeled red potato	2 cups	500 mL
Chopped onion	2 cups	500 mL
Diced celery	1 cup	250 mL
Can of tomato paste	5 1/2 oz.	156 mL
Diced carrot	1/2 cup	125 mL
Bacon slices, cooked crisp and crumbled	5	5
Dried thyme	1 tsp.	5 mL
Cayenne pepper	1/4 tsp.	1 mL

Drain clam liquid into 5 to 7 quart (5 to 7 L) slow cooker. Cover and
chill clams.

Add remaining 10 ingredients to slow cooker. Cook, covered, on Low for
8 to 10 hours or on High for 4 to 5 hours until vegetables are very tender.
Add clams. Stir well. Cook, covered, on High for about 10 minutes until
heated through. Makes about 14 cups (3.5 L).

*1 cup (250 mL): 83 Calories; 1.7 g Total Fat (0.6 g Mono, 0.3 g Poly, 0.5 g Sat); 10 mg Cholesterol;
12 g Carbohydrate; 2 g Fibre; 6 g Protein; 199 mg Sodium*

1. Pumpkin Blue Cheese Soup, page 91
2. Roasted Vegetable Chowder, page 64
3. Fresh Garden Chowder, page 76

Props courtesy of: The Bay
Casa Bugatti
Cherison Enterprises Inc.

Minted Green Pea Chowder

If you could cook up summer, it would taste like this! Fresh mint and sweet peas make this elegant soup unique both in flavour and appearance.

Butter (or hard margarine)	3 tbsp.	50 mL
Chopped onion	1 cup	250 mL
Diced peeled potato	1 cup	250 mL
Vegetable (or chicken) stock	4 cups	1 L
Fresh (or frozen) peas	2 cups	500 mL
Half-and-half cream	1/2 cup	125 mL
Chopped fresh mint	1/4 cup	60 mL

Melt butter in large saucepan on medium. Add onion. Cook for 5 to 10 minutes, stirring often, until softened.

Add potato and stock. Bring to a boil. Reduce heat to medium-low. Simmer, partially covered, on medium-low for 10 minutes.

Add peas. Return to a boil. Cook for about 3 minutes, stirring occasionally, until potato is tender. Remove from heat. Remove 1 cup (250 mL) of pea mixture with slotted spoon to small bowl. Set aside.

Add cream and mint to saucepan. Stir. Carefully process in blender until smooth (see Safety Tip). Return to saucepan. Add reserved pea mixture. Heat and stir on medium until heated through. Makes about 6 1/2 cups (1.6 L).

1 cup (250 mL): 146 Calories; 7.9 g Total Fat (2.2 g Mono, 0.4 g Poly, 4.9 g Sat); 21 mg Cholesterol; 15 g Carbohydrate; 3 g Fibre; 5 g Protein; 646 mg Sodium

Pictured on page 18.

Safety Tip: Follow manufacturer's instructions for processing hot liquids.

1. Chicken Fennel Chowder, page 79
2. Creamy Kale Soup, page 98
3. Pepper Pot Chowder, page 77

Props courtesy of: Casa Bugatti

Autumn Chowder

It's that thyme of the year. Fresh thyme enhances a medley of vegetable flavours—perfect for lunch on a cool autumn day.

Cooking oil	2 tbsp.	30 mL
Chopped onion	1 1/2 cups	375 mL
Garlic clove, minced (or 1/4 tsp., 1 mL, powder)	1	1
All-purpose flour	3 tbsp.	50 mL
Chicken (or vegetable) stock	4 cups	1 L
Chopped red baby potato	2 cups	500 mL
Chopped carrot	1 1/2 cups	375 mL
Chopped fennel bulb (white part only)	1 cup	250 mL
Chopped red pepper	1 cup	250 mL
Sprigs of fresh thyme	4 – 5	4 – 5
Frozen kernel corn	1 cup	250 mL
Salt, sprinkle		
Pepper, sprinkle		

Heat cooking oil in large saucepan on medium. Add onion and garlic. Cook for 5 to 10 minutes, stirring often, until onion is softened.

Sprinkle with flour. Heat and stir for 1 minute.

Slowly add 2 cups (500 mL) stock. Heat and stir until boiling and thickened. Add remaining stock and next 5 ingredients. Stir. Bring to a boil. Reduce heat to medium-low. Simmer, covered, for 15 to 20 minutes, stirring occasionally, until potato is tender. Discard thyme sprigs.

Add remaining 3 ingredients. Cook for about 3 minutes, stirring occasionally, until corn is heated through. Makes about 8 cups (2 L).

1 cup (250 mL): 133 Calories; 4.1 g Total Fat (2.1 g Mono, 1.2 g Poly, 0.6 g Sat); 0 mg Cholesterol; 22 g Carbohydrate; 3 g Fibre; 4 g Protein; 460 mg Sodium

Lemon Parsnip Chowder

"Zing, zing, zing went my heartstrings!" Tangy fresh lemon zest and a hint of nutmeg round out a wonderful roasted parsnip flavour.

Diced parsnip	2 cups	500 mL
Diced carrot	1 cup	250 mL
Olive (or cooking oil)	1 tsp.	5 mL
Bacon slices, diced	3	3
Sliced leek (white part only)	2 cups	500 mL
Diced peeled potatoes	2 cups	500 mL
Water	2 cups	500 mL
Can of condensed chicken broth	10 oz.	284 mL
Grated lemon zest	1 tsp.	5 mL
Ground nutmeg	1/8 tsp.	0.5 mL
Sour cream	1/4 cup	60 mL

Put parsnip and carrot into medium bowl. Drizzle with olive oil. Stir until coated. Arrange in single layer on ungreased baking sheet with sides. Bake in 425°F (220°C) oven for about 15 minutes until tender-crisp and starting to brown. Set aside.

Cook bacon in large saucepan on medium until almost crisp. Drain all but 1 tsp. (5 mL) drippings. Add leek. Cook for 3 to 5 minutes, stirring occasionally, until softened.

Add next 5 ingredients and roasted vegetables. Stir. Bring to a boil. Reduce heat to medium-low. Simmer, partially covered, for 15 to 20 minutes, stirring occasionally, until potato is tender. Remove from heat.

Add sour cream. Stir. Makes about 6 cups (1.5 L).

1 cup (250 mL): 175 Calories; 5.4 g Total Fat (2.3 g Mono, 0.6 g Poly, 2.1 g Sat); 8 mg Cholesterol; 27 g Carbohydrate; 4 g Fibre; 6 g Protein; 403 mg Sodium

Fresh Garden Chowder

Tangy feta and fresh dill enhance the flavours of hearty vegetables. Make this soup after you harvest your garden and enjoy that fresh, home-grown vegetable flavour.

Cooking oil	1 1/2 tbsp.	25 mL
Chopped zucchini (with peel)	1 1/2 cups	375 mL
Chopped onion	1 cup	250 mL
Chopped celery	1/2 cup	125 mL
All-purpose flour	2 tbsp.	30 mL
Chicken (or vegetable) stock	3 cups	750 mL
Chopped peeled potato	2 cups	500 mL
Fresh spinach leaves, lightly packed, chopped	2 cups	500 mL
Milk	1 cup	250 mL
Chopped fresh dill (or 3/4 tsp., 4 mL, dill weed)	1 tbsp.	15 mL
Salt	1/4 tsp.	1 mL
Pepper	1/8 tsp.	0.5 mL
Crumbled feta cheese	1/4 cup	60 mL

Heat cooking oil in large saucepan on medium. Add next 3 ingredients. Cook for about 10 minutes, stirring often, until onion is softened.

Sprinkle with flour. Heat and stir for 1 minute.

Slowly add 1 cup (250 mL) stock. Heat and stir until boiling and thickened. Add potato and remaining stock. Stir. Bring to a boil. Reduce heat to medium-low. Simmer, partially covered, for 15 to 20 minutes, stirring occasionally, until potato is tender.

Add next 5 ingredients. Stir. Cook for about 2 minutes until spinach is wilted. Carefully transfer 3 cups (750 mL) of soup to blender. Process until smooth (see Safety Tip). Return to saucepan. Heat and stir until heated through.

Sprinkle feta cheese on individual servings. Makes about 6 1/2 cups (1.6 L).

1 cup (250 mL): 137 Calories; 5.4 g Total Fat (2.3 g Mono, 1.1 g Poly, 1.7 g Sat); 7 mg Cholesterol; 18 g Carbohydrate; 2 g Fibre; 5 g Protein; 606 mg Sodium

Pictured on page 71.

Safety Tip: Follow manufacturer's instructions for processing hot liquids.

Pepper Pot Chowder

Colourful fresh peppers abound in this golden chowder. Use your favourite variety of hot chili pepper for your preferred heat level.

Cooking oil	1 tsp.	5 mL
Chopped onion	1 cup	250 mL
Chopped celery	1/2 cup	125 mL
Garlic cloves, minced (or 1/2 tsp, 2 mL, powder)	2	2
Fresh hot chili peppers, seeds and ribs removed (see Tip, page 26), finely chopped	2	2
Vegetable (or chicken) stock	5 cups	1.25 L
Diced peeled potato	2 cups	500 mL
Diced green pepper	1 cup	250 mL
Diced red pepper	1 cup	250 mL
Diced yellow or orange pepper (optional)	1/2 cup	125 ml
Chopped fresh parsley	1/4 cup	60 mL
Chopped fresh thyme	2 tsp.	10 mL
Salt	1/4 tsp.	1 mL
Pepper	1/4 tsp.	1 mL

Heat cooking oil in large saucepan on medium. Add next 4 ingredients. Cook for 5 to 10 minutes, stirring often, until onion is softened.

Add stock and potato. Bring to a boil. Reduce heat to medium-low. Simmer, partially covered, for 15 to 20 minutes, stirring occasionally, until potato is tender (see Note).

Add remaining 7 ingredients. Stir. Simmer, uncovered, for 5 to 7 minutes until peppers are tender-crisp. Makes about 8 cups (2 L).

1 cup (250 mL): 73 Calories; 1.1 g Total Fat (0.4 g Mono, 0.3 g Poly, 0.4 g Sat); 0 mg Cholesterol; 14 g Carbohydrate; 2 g Fibre; 3 g Protein; 623 mg Sodium

Pictured on page 72.

Note: For a thicker soup, potatoes may be slightly mashed prior to adding remaining 7 ingredients.

Turkey And Bacon Chowder

Imagine the perfect turkey sandwich with bacon and a creamy, mild Dijon. Now imagine those same flavours in a hale and hearty chowder. Need we say more?

Bacon slices, diced	5	5
Lean ground turkey	1/2 lb.	225 g
Sliced fresh white mushrooms	2 1/2 cups	625 mL
Chopped onion	1/2 cup	125 mL
Chopped celery	1/2 cup	125 mL
Finely chopped green onion	1/4 cup	60 mL
Diced red pepper	1/4 cup	60 mL
Turkey (or chicken) stock	5 cups	1.25 L
Chopped unpeeled red potato	3 cups	750 mL
Dried thyme	1/2 tsp.	2 mL
Salt	1/2 tsp.	2 mL
Pepper	1/4 tsp.	1 mL
Frozen kernel corn	1/2 cup	125 mL
All-purpose flour	1/4 cup	60 mL
Skim evaporated milk	3/4 cup	175 mL
Dijon mustard	1 tbsp.	15 mL

Cook bacon in large saucepan on medium until crisp. Transfer with slotted spoon to paper towels to drain. Set aside.

Heat 1 tbsp. (15 mL) drippings in same saucepan on medium. Add turkey. Scramble-fry for about 5 minutes until no longer pink.

Add next 5 ingredients. Cook for about 5 minutes, stirring occasionally, until vegetables are softened.

Add next 5 ingredients. Stir. Bring to a boil. Reduce heat to medium-low. Simmer, covered, for 15 to 20 minutes, stirring occasionally, until potato is tender.

Add corn and bacon. Stir.

Stir remaining 3 ingredients with whisk in small bowl until smooth. Slowly stir into soup. Heat and stir on medium for about 5 minutes until boiling and slightly thickened. Makes about 9 cups (2.25 L).

1 cup (250 mL): 172 Calories; 6.0 g Total Fat (2.3 g Mono, 1.1 g Poly, 2.1 g Sat); 25 mg Cholesterol; 20 g Carbohydrate; 2 g Fibre; 11 g Protein; 749 mg Sodium

Pictured on page 144.

Chicken Fennel Chowder

*Here's a robust and satisfying chowder with smoky bacon, hearty
chunks of chicken and a dash of cayenne for that extra kick.
Garnish with diced red pepper and fresh thyme.*

Bacon slices, diced	4	4
Boneless, skinless chicken breast halves, chopped	1 lb.	454 g
Finely chopped red onion	1 cup	250 mL
Finely chopped red pepper	1 cup	250 mL
Finely chopped fennel bulb (white part only)	1/2 cup	125 mL
All-purpose flour	1/4 cup	60 mL
Chicken stock	3 cups	750 mL
Chopped peeled potato	1 1/2 cups	375 mL
Skim evaporated milk	3/4 cup	175 mL
Chopped fresh thyme (or 1/4 tsp., 1 mL, dried)	1 1/2 tsp.	7 mL
Cayenne pepper	1/4 tsp.	1 mL

Cook bacon in large saucepan on medium until almost crisp. Transfer with
slotted spoon to paper towels to drain. Set aside.

Heat 1 tbsp. (15 mL) drippings in same saucepan on medium-high. Add
chicken. Cook for 3 minutes, stirring occasionally.

Add next 3 ingredients. Cook for about 10 minutes, stirring often, until
chicken is no longer pink inside and onion is softened. Reduce heat
to medium.

Add flour. Heat and stir for 1 minute.

Add stock, stirring constantly, scraping any brown bits from bottom of pan.
Add potato. Bring to a boil. Reduce heat to medium. Boil gently, partially
covered, for 15 to 20 minutes, stirring occasionally, until potato is tender.

Add bacon and remaining 3 ingredients. Heat and stir until heated through.
Makes about 5 1/2 cups (1.4 L).

*1 cup (250 mL): 253 Calories; 6.6 g Total Fat (2.5 g Mono, 1.0 g Poly, 2.5 g Sat); 55 mg Cholesterol;
22 g Carbohydrate; 2 g Fibre; 26 g Protein; 589 mg Sodium*

Pictured on page 72.

Pastry-Topped Chicken Chowder

The puff pastry crust makes this dish pure bliss! Sure to impress your most special guests. Serve without the crust, if you're so inclined.

Cooking oil	2 tsp.	10 mL
Boneless, skinless chicken breast halves, cut into 1/2 inch (12 mm) cubes	6 oz.	170 g
Diced peeled potato	1 cup	250 mL
Chopped fresh white mushrooms	1 cup	250 mL
Garlic cloves, minced (or 1/2 tsp., 2 mL, powder)	2	2
Salt	1/2 tsp.	2 mL
Pepper	1/2 tsp.	2 mL
Dried crushed chilies	1/4 tsp.	1 mL
All-purpose flour	1 tbsp.	15 mL
Tomato paste (see Tip, page 49)	1 tbsp.	15 mL
Dried tarragon	1/2 tsp.	2 mL
Chicken stock	2 1/2 cups	625 mL
Sun-dried tomatoes in oil, blotted dry, chopped	1/3 cup	75 mL
Balsamic vinegar	2 tbsp.	30 mL
Whipping cream	1/2 cup	125 mL
Chopped green onion	1/3 cup	75 mL
Package of puff pastry (14 oz., 397 g), thawed according to package directions	1/2	1/2
Large egg, fork-beaten	1	1

Heat cooking oil in large saucepan on medium. Add chicken. Cook for about 5 minutes, stirring occasionally, until no longer pink inside.

Add next 6 ingredients. Cook for about 5 minutes, stirring occasionally, until mushrooms release liquid.

Add next 3 ingredients. Heat and stir for 1 minute.

(continued on next page)

Add next 3 ingredients. Heat and stir until boiling. Reduce heat to medium-low. Simmer, covered, for 15 to 20 minutes, stirring occasionally, until potato is tender.

Add cream and green onion. Stir. Makes about 5 cups (1.25 L). Ladle into six 1 cup (250 mL) ovenproof ramekins. Place on baking sheet with sides. Set aside.

Roll out puff pastry on lightly floured surface to 10 × 15 inch (25 cm × 37 cm) rectangle. Cut into six 5 inch (12.5 cm) squares. (See Note)

Brush top rim of ramekins with egg. Place 1 pastry square over each ramekin. Press pastry to ramekins to seal. Gently brush egg on pastry. Bake in 400°F (205°C) oven for about 20 minutes until pastry is puffed and golden. Serves 6.

1 serving: 360 Calories; 23.4 g Total Fat (6.8 g Mono, 8.3 g Poly, 6.8 g Sat); 77 mg Cholesterol; 26 g Carbohydrate; trace Fibre; 13 g Protein; 695 mg Sodium

Pictured on page 90 and on back cover.

Note: For easy rolling, puff pastry should be cool. Always wrap pastry in plastic wrap if not using immediately.

Paré Pointer
Crossing an electric blanket with a toaster would make you pop out of bed every morning.

Boston Clam Chowder

You don't have to be from Boston to make a charming chowder—all you need is the recipe! Dill adds a fresh accent to the clam and smoky bacon flavours.

Bacon slices, diced	4	4
Chopped onion	1 cup	250 mL
Diced celery	1/2 cup	125 mL
All-purpose flour	1/4 cup	60 mL
Cans of whole baby clams (5 oz., 142 g each)	2	2
Water	1 cup	250 mL
Diced peeled potato	3 cups	750 mL
Bay leaf	1	1
Salt	1/2 tsp.	2 mL
Pepper	1/4 tsp.	1 mL
Ground thyme	1/4 tsp.	1 mL
Milk	2 cups	500 mL
Chopped fresh dill (or 1 1/2 tsp., 7 mL, dill weed)	2 tbsp.	30 mL

Cook bacon in large saucepan on medium until almost crisp. Add onion and celery. Cook for about 5 minutes, stirring occasionally, until onion is softened.

Sprinkle with flour. Heat and stir for 1 minute.

Drain clams, reserving 1 cup (250 mL) liquid. Cover and chill clams. Add clam liquid and water to saucepan. Heat and stir until boiling and thickened.

Add next 5 ingredients. Stir. Bring to a boil. Reduce heat to medium-low. Simmer, covered, for about 20 minutes, stirring occasionally, until potato is tender.

Add clams, milk and dill. Cook for about 5 minutes, stirring often, until heated through. Discard bay leaf. Makes about 8 cups (2 L).

1 cup (250 mL): 204 Calories; 6.7 g Total Fat (4.0 g Mono, 1.2 g Poly, 3.5 g Sat); 35 mg Cholesterol; 21 g Carbohydrate; 2 g Fibre; 15 g Protein; 372 mg Sodium

Carrot Satay Soup

*Don't tie yourself to the stove—this Thai delight is made in
your slow cooker. Creamy carrots, peanut undertones and
a gentle spicy heat make this soup vibrant and velvety.*

Chicken stock	3 cups	750 mL
Sliced carrot	3 cups	750 mL
Chopped onion	1 cup	250 mL
Chopped celery	1/2 cup	125 mL
Brown sugar, packed	2 tbsp.	30 mL
Garlic cloves, minced (or 1/2 tsp., 2 mL, powder)	2	2
Finely grated ginger root	2 tsp.	10 mL
Salt	1/2 tsp.	2 mL
Cayenne pepper	1/8 tsp.	0.5 mL
Cream cheese, softened	1/4 cup	60 mL
Smooth peanut butter	3 tbsp.	50 mL
Soy sauce	1 tbsp.	15 mL
Sesame seeds, toasted (see Tip), for garnish		

Combine first 9 ingredients in 3 1/2 to 4 quart (3.5 to 4 L) slow cooker.
Cook, covered, on Low for 5 to 6 hours or on High for 2 1/2 to 3 hours
until vegetables are tender.

Add remaining 3 ingredients. Carefully process with hand blender or in
blender until smooth (see Safety Tip).

Garnish individual servings with sesame seeds. Makes about 6 cups (1.5 L).

*1 cup (250 mL): 164 Calories; 8.2 g Total Fat (3.0 g Mono, 1.4 g Poly, 3.4 g Sat); 11 mg Cholesterol;
19 g Carbohydrate; 3 g Fibre; 5 g Protein; 936 mg Sodium*

Pictured on page 35.

Safety Tip: Follow manufacturer's instructions for processing
hot liquids.

 To toast nuts, seeds or coconut, place them in an ungreased shallow
frying pan. Heat on medium for 3 to 5 minutes, stirring often, until
golden. To bake, spread them evenly in an ungreased shallow pan.
Bake in a 350°F (175°C) oven for 5 to 10 minutes, stirring or shaking
often, until golden.

Jasmine Leek Bisque

Can a soup taste pretty? Indeed! The gentle flavours of leek and fragrant jasmine rice combine in a uniquely textured, velvety soup.

Cooking oil	2 tsp.	10 mL
Chopped leek (white part only)	2 1/2 cups	625 mL
Chopped celery	1 cup	250 mL
Garlic cloves, minced (or 1/2 tsp., 2 mL, powder)	2	2
Chicken (or vegetable) stock	4 cups	1 L
Water	1 1/2 cups	375 mL
Jasmine rice	1/2 cup	125 mL
CLASSIC BOUQUET GARNI		
Sprigs of fresh parsley	4	4
Sprigs of fresh thyme	4	4
Bay leaf	1	1
Half-and-half cream	1/4 cup	60 mL

Heat cooking oil in large saucepan on medium. Add next 3 ingredients. Cook for about 5 minutes, stirring occasionally, until leek is softened.

Add next 3 ingredients. Stir.

Classic Bouquet Garni: Place first 3 ingredients on 10 inch (25 cm) square piece of cheesecloth. Draw up corners and tie with butcher's string. Submerge in stock mixture. Bring to a boil. Reduce heat to medium-low. Simmer, covered, for about 20 minutes, stirring occasionally, until rice is tender. Discard bouquet garni. Carefully process with hand blender or in blender until smooth (see Safety Tip).

Add cream. Heat and stir until heated through. Makes about 7 cups (1.75 L).

1 cup (250 mL): 111 Calories; 2.8 g Total Fat (1.0 g Mono, 0.5 g Poly, 1.0 g Sat); 3 mg Cholesterol; 19 g Carbohydrate; 1 g Fibre; 3 g Protein; 519 mg Sodium

Safety Tip: Follow manufacturer's instructions for processing hot liquids.

Gingered Carrot Soup

This carrot purée snaps to attention with the addition
of spicy ginger. Garnish with sliced green onion.

Butter (or hard margarine)	1 tbsp.	15 mL
Chopped carrot	2 cups	500 mL
Chopped onion	1 cup	250 mL
Chopped celery	1/2 cup	125 mL
Finely grated ginger root	2 tbsp.	30 mL
Chicken (or vegetable) stock	3 cups	750 mL
Long grain brown rice	1/4 cup	60 mL
Liquid honey	1 tbsp.	15 mL
Salt	1/4 tsp.	1 mL
Pepper	1/4 tsp.	1 mL

Melt butter in large saucepan on medium. Add next 4 ingredients. Cook for 5 to 10 minutes, stirring occasionally, until onion is softened.

Add remaining 5 ingredients. Bring to a boil. Reduce heat to medium-low. Simmer, covered, for about 50 minutes, stirring occasionally, until rice is tender. Carefully process with hand blender or in blender until smooth (see Safety Tip). Makes about 4 cups (1 L).

1 cup (250 mL): 158 Calories; 3.9 g Total Fat (1.0 g Mono, 0.4 g Poly, 2.3 g Sat); 8 mg Cholesterol; 29 g Carbohydrate; 4 g Fibre; 4 g Protein; 893 mg Sodium

Pictured on page 18.

Safety Tip: Follow manufacturer's instructions for processing hot liquids.

Paré Pointer
He works for a good cause—'cause he needs the money.

Roasted Garlic Spinach Soup

Even kids will eat their spinach when you serve them this silky cream soup flavoured with roasted garlic and pesto. Factor in extra time to roast the garlic.

Garlic bulbs	2	2
Cooking oil	1 tsp.	5 mL
Chopped onion	1 cup	250 mL
All-purpose flour	1/4 cup	60 mL
Chicken stock	4 cups	1 L
Water	1 cup	250 mL
Pepper	1/2 tsp.	2 mL
Fresh spinach leaves, lightly packed	6 cups	1.5 L
Basil pesto	2 tbsp.	30 mL
Grated Parmesan cheese	1/2 cup	125 mL
Whipping cream	1/2 cup	125 mL

Trim 1/4 inch (6 mm) from garlic bulbs to expose tops of cloves, leaving bulbs intact. Wrap loosely in greased foil. Bake in 375°F (190°C) oven for about 45 minutes until tender. Let stand until cool enough to handle. Squeeze garlic bulb to remove cloves from peel. Discard peel. Set aside.

Heat cooking oil in large saucepan on medium. Add onion. Cook for 5 to 10 minutes, stirring occasionally, until onion is softened.

Add flour. Heat and stir for 1 minute.

Slowly add 2 cups (500 mL) stock. Heat and stir until boiling and thickened. Add water, pepper and remaining stock. Stir. Add roasted garlic. Bring to a boil, stirring with whisk.

Add spinach and pesto. Cook for about 5 minutes until spinach is very soft. Carefully process with hand blender or in blender until smooth (see Safety Tip).

Add Parmesan cheese and cream. Heat and stir for about 2 minutes until heated through. Makes about 7 cups (1.75 L).

1 cup (250 mL): 169 Calories; 10.6 g Total Fat (3.7 g Mono, 0.7 g Poly, 5.6 g Sat); 27 mg Cholesterol; 13 g Carbohydrate; 2 g Fibre; 7 g Protein; 680 mg Sodium

Safety Tip: Follow manufacturer's instructions for processing hot liquids.

Curried Cauliflower Soup

Truly the bee's knees! Honey adds a delicate sweetness to the creamy curry flavour of this delightful golden purée.

Cooking oil	2 tbsp.	30 mL
Chopped onion	2 cups	500 mL
Chopped carrot	1 cup	250 mL
Garlic cloves, minced (or 1/2 tsp., 2 mL, powder)	2	2
Finely grated gingerroot	2 tsp.	10 mL
Curry powder	1 tbsp.	15 mL
All-purpose flour	1/4 cup	60 mL
Chicken (or vegetable) stock	4 cups	1 L
Chopped cauliflower	5 cups	1.25 L
Can of 2% evaporated milk	13 1/2 oz.	385 mL
Salt	1/4 tsp.	1 mL
Liquid honey	3 tbsp.	50 mL

Heat cooking oil in large saucepan on medium. Add next 4 ingredients. Cook for 5 to 10 minutes, stirring often, until onion is softened.

Add curry powder. Heat and stir for about 1 minute until vegetables are coated and curry is fragrant.

Sprinkle with flour. Heat and stir for 1 minute.

Slowly stir in 2 cups (500 mL) stock, scraping any brown bits from bottom of pan, until boiling and thickened. Add remaining stock and next 3 ingredients. Stir. Bring to a boil. Reduce heat to medium-low. Simmer, uncovered, for about 15 minutes, stirring occasionally, until cauliflower is tender.

Add honey. Carefully process with hand blender or in blender until smooth (see Safety Tip). Makes about 8 1/2 cups (2.1 L).

1 cup (250 mL): 150 Calories; 4.8 g Total Fat (2.2 g Mono, 1.1 g Poly, 1.1 g Sat); 4 mg Cholesterol; 22 g Carbohydrate; 3 g Fibre; 7 g Protein; 561 mg Sodium

Safety Tip: Follow manufacturer's instructions for processing hot liquids.

Roasted Tomato Soup

When fall comes don't be overrun by your garden bounty of tomatoes.
Reclaim your space by roasting them in great abandon.
The result will be a delectably tangy soup.

Medium tomatoes, chopped	10	10
Chopped onion	1/2 cup	125 mL
Garlic cloves, minced	2	2
Olive (or cooking) oil	2 tsp.	10 mL
Granulated sugar	1 tsp.	5 mL
Balsamic vinegar	1/2 tsp.	2 mL
Salt	1/4 tsp.	1 mL
Pepper	1/8 tsp.	0.5 mL
Chicken (or vegetable) stock	2 cups	500 mL
Sour cream	2 tbsp.	30 mL

Combine first 8 ingredients in large bowl. Spread evenly in ungreased baking sheet with sides. Bake in 350°F (175°C) oven for about 1 hour until tomato is softened and juices are bubbling. Cool slightly. Transfer to blender.

Add 1 cup (250 mL) stock to blender. Process until smooth (see Safety Tip). Pour into large saucepan (see Note). Add sour cream and remaining stock. Stir with whisk until smooth. Heat on medium for about 15 minutes, stirring often, until hot but not boiling. Makes about 6 cups (1.5 L).

1 cup (250 mL): 92 Calories; 3.2 g Total Fat (1.5 g Mono, 0.5 g Poly, 0.9 g Sat); 2 mg Cholesterol; 15 g Carbohydrate; 3 g Fibre; 3 g Protein; 411 mg Sodium

Safety Tip: Follow manufacturer's instructions for processing hot liquids.
Note: Strain vegetable mixture after processing to remove tomato seeds and skin if desired.

1. Shrimp Bisque, page 50
2. Cream Of Mushroom Soup, page 103

Props courtesy of: Pfaltzgraff Canada

Pumpkin Blue Cheese Soup

Pumpkins aren't just for jack-o-lanterns any more.
Don't wait until Halloween to make this rich
soup—it's so easy to prepare, it's spooky!

Chicken stock	2 cups	500 mL
Can of pure pumpkin (no spices)	14 oz.	398 mL
Ground sage	1/2 tsp.	2 mL
Pepper	1/4 tsp.	1 mL
Can of evaporated milk	13 1/2 oz.	385 mL
Crumbled blue cheese	1/2 cup	125 mL

Chopped fresh chives, for garnish

Combine first 4 ingredients in large saucepan. Bring to a boil on medium, stirring often.

Add evaporated milk and cheese. Stir. Reduce heat to low. Cook, uncovered, for about 5 minutes, stirring often, until cheese is melted and soup is hot but not boiling.

Garnish individual servings with chives. Makes about 5 cups (1.25 L).

1 cup (250 mL): 194 Calories; 10.8 g Total Fat (3.1 g Mono, 0.3 g Poly, 6.8 g Sat); 34 mg Cholesterol; 16 g Carbohydrate; 2 g Fibre; 10 g Protein; 631 mg Sodium

Pictured on page 71.

Safety Tip: Follow manufacturer's instructions for processing hot liquids.

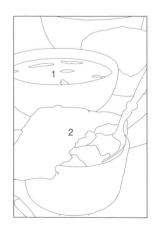

1. Crab Asparagus Soup, page 102
2. Pastry-Topped Chicken Chowder, page 80

Props courtesy of: Call the Kettle Black
Danesco Inc.
Dansk Gifts

Creamy Garden Soup

*This fresh veggie and cheese soup is sure to warm you
from the top of your head to the tips of your toes.*

Butter (or hard margarine)	2 tbsp.	30 mL
Chopped onion	1 cup	250 mL
Garlic clove, minced (or 1/4 tsp., 1 mL, powder)	1	1
Water	2 1/2 cups	625 mL
Chopped broccoli	2 cups	500 mL
Diced carrot	1/2 cup	125 mL
Milk	1 cup	250 mL
Small cauliflower florets	1 cup	250 mL
Small broccoli florets	1 cup	250 mL
Diced carrot	1/2 cup	125 mL
Dry mustard	1/2 tsp.	2 mL
Dill weed	1/2 tsp.	2 mL
Salt	1/2 tsp.	2 mL
Pepper	1/4 tsp.	1 mL
Diced zucchini (with peel)	1/2 cup	125 mL
Frozen peas	1/2 cup	125 mL
Grated sharp Cheddar cheese	1 cup	250 mL
Lemon juice	1 tbsp.	15 mL

Melt butter in large saucepan on medium. Add onion and garlic. Cook for
5 to 10 minutes, stirring often, until onion is softened.

Add next 3 ingredients. Stir. Bring to a boil. Reduce heat to medium-low.
Simmer, covered, for about 10 minutes until vegetables are tender. Carefully
process with hand blender or in blender until smooth (see Safety Tip).

Add next 8 ingredients. Bring to a boil. Reduce heat to medium-low.
Simmer, uncovered, for about 10 minutes until vegetables are tender-crisp.

Add zucchini and peas. Cook for about 5 minutes, stirring occasionally,
until zucchini is tender-crisp.

Add cheese and lemon juice. Heat and stir until cheese is melted. Makes
about 5 1/2 cups (1.4 L).

*1 cup (250 mL): 205 Calories; 12.4 g Total Fat (3.5 g Mono, 0.6 g Poly, 7.6 g Sat); 36 mg Cholesterol;
15 g Carbohydrate; 4 g Fibre; 11 g Protein; 474 mg Sodium*

Safety Tip: Follow manufacturer's instructions for processing hot liquids.

Dill Pickle Soup

You're never in a pickle when you serve this fun and festive soup. Perfect served with grilled cheese sandwiches. Try adding cooked diced chicken, ham or sausage for extra protein.

Butter (or hard margarine)	2 tbsp.	30 mL
Chopped peeled potato	2 cups	500 mL
Chopped onion	1 cup	250 mL
Chopped carrot	1 cup	250 mL
Pepper	1/4 tsp.	1 mL
All-purpose flour	2 tbsp.	30 mL
Chicken stock	4 cups	1 L
Dill pickle juice	1/4 cup	60 mL
Half-and-half cream	1 cup	250 mL
Chopped dill pickles	2/3 cup	150 mL
Chopped fresh dill (or 1 tbsp., 15 mL, dill weed)	1/4 cup	60 mL
Sour cream	1/2 cup	125 mL

Melt butter in large saucepan on medium. Add next 4 ingredients. Stir. Cook, partially covered, for 8 to 10 minutes, stirring occasionally, until vegetables start to soften.

Sprinkle with flour. Heat and stir for 1 minute.

Slowly add 1 cup (250 mL) stock. Heat and stir until boiling and thickened. Add pickle juice and remaining stock. Cook, stirring often, until boiling. Reduce heat to medium-low. Simmer, covered, for about 15 minutes, stirring occasionally, until potato is tender.

Add cream and pickles. Stir. Cook for about 2 minutes until hot but not boiling. Add dill. Carefully process with hand blender or in blender until smooth (see Safety Tip).

Spoon sour cream onto individual servings. Makes about 8 cups (2 L).

1 cup (250 mL): 152 Calories; 8.6 g Total Fat (2.4 g Mono, 0.4 g Poly, 5.4 g Sat); 24 mg Cholesterol; 16 g Carbohydrate; 2 g Fibre; 4 g Protein; 623 mg Sodium

Safety Tip: Follow manufacturer's instructions for processing hot liquids.

Garden Fresh Tomato Soup

Forget the canned tomatoes, this soup is a tangy treat full of fresh veggies to eat. Great for when your kitchen is overflowing with all your harvested garden tomatoes.

Medium tomatoes (about 3 lbs., 1.4 kg)	8	8
Cooking oil	2 tsp.	10 mL
Chopped onion	1 cup	250 mL
Chopped carrot	1/2 cup	125 mL
Chopped celery	1/2 cup	125 mL
Garlic cloves, minced (or 1/2 tsp., 2 mL, powder)	2	2
Chicken (or vegetable) stock	1 cup	250 mL
Tomato paste (see Tip, page 49)	2 tbsp.	30 mL
Granulated sugar	2 tsp.	10 mL
Dried basil	1/2 tsp.	2 mL
Dried oregano	1/2 tsp.	2 mL
Dried thyme	1/2 tsp.	2 mL
Bay leaf	1	1
Salt	1/2 tsp.	2 mL
Pepper	1/2 tsp.	2 mL

Cut 'X' through skin on bottom of tomatoes. Place tomatoes in boiling water in large saucepan for 30 seconds. Transfer to ice water in large bowl using slotted spoon. Let stand until cool enough to handle. Peel and discard skins. Cut each tomato into quarters. Remove seeds. Chop tomato. Set aside. Discard cooking water.

Heat cooking oil in same saucepan on medium. Add next 4 ingredients. Cook for 5 to 10 minutes, stirring occasionally, until vegetables are softened.

Add tomato and remaining 9 ingredients. Stir. Bring to a boil. Reduce heat to medium-low. Simmer, covered, for about 30 minutes, stirring occasionally, until vegetables are very soft. Discard bay leaf. Carefully process with hand blender or in blender until smooth (see Safety Tip). Makes about 5 cups (1.25 L).

1 cup (250 mL): 114 Calories; 3.0 g Total Fat (1.3 g Mono, 1.0 g Poly, 0.4 g Sat); 0 mg Cholesterol; 22 g Carbohydrate; 5 g Fibre; 4 g Protein; 461 mg Sodium

Safety Tip: Follow manufacturer's instructions for processing hot liquids.

CREAM OF TOMATO SOUP: Add 1/2 cup (125 mL) whipping cream after processing. Heat and stir until heated through.

Cream Of Spinach Soup

A touch of nutmeg contrasts nicely with the rich, earthy flavour of spinach.

Cooking oil	1 tbsp.	15 mL
Chopped onion	1 1/2 cups	375 mL
Garlic cloves, minced (or 1/2 tsp., 2 mL, powder)	2	2
All-purpose flour	2 tbsp.	30 mL
Ground nutmeg	1/8 tsp.	0.5 mL
Chicken (or vegetable) stock	4 cups	1 L
Fresh spinach leaves, lightly packed	4 cups	1 L
Pepper	1/4 tsp.	1 mL
Half-and-half cream (or evaporated milk)	1/2 cup	125 mL

Heat cooking oil in large saucepan on medium. Add onion and garlic. Cook for 5 to 10 minutes, stirring often, until onion is softened.

Add flour and nutmeg. Heat and stir for 1 minute.

Slowly add 1 cup (250 mL) stock. Heat and stir until boiling and thickened. Add remaining stock. Cook for about 10 minutes, stirring often, until boiling.

Add spinach and pepper. Heat and stir for about 2 minutes until spinach is wilted. Carefully process with hand blender or in blender until smooth (see Safety Tip).

Add cream. Heat and stir for 2 to 3 minutes until heated through. Makes about 5 cups (1.25 L).

1 cup (250 mL): 111 Calories; 6.0 g Total Fat (2.4 g Mono, 1.0 g Poly, 2.2 g Sat); 8 mg Cholesterol; 11 g Carbohydrate; 2 g Fibre; 4 g Protein; 736 mg Sodium

Safety Tip: Follow manufacturer's instructions for processing hot liquids.

Paré Pointer
The best-read garden magazine is The Weeder's Digest.

Roasted Yam Cream Soup

Cardamom, a spice commonly used in Eastern countries, adds a pleasant lemony flavour to curries, rice dishes and desserts. Here, cardamom-flavoured sour cream adds a special touch to a smooth puréed soup—after all, it's the simple, little touches that show you care!

CARDAMOM CREAM

Sour cream	1/2 cup	125 mL
Ground cardamom	1/2 tsp.	2 mL

SOUP

Unpeeled yam (or sweet potato) cut into 1/2 inch (12 mm) slices	1 lb.	454 g
Carrots, cut into 1/2 inch (12 mm) slices	1/2 lb.	225 g
Unpeeled garlic cloves	4	4
Olive (or cooking) oil	1 tbsp.	15 mL
Olive (or cooking) oil	1 tsp.	5 mL
Chopped leek (white part only)	1 cup	250 mL
Finely grated ginger root	1 tsp.	5 mL
Chicken (or vegetable) stock	5 cups	1.25 L
Salt	1/4 tsp.	1 mL
Pepper	1/8 tsp.	0.5 mL
Half-and-half cream	1/2 cup	125 mL

Cardamom Cream: Combine sour cream and cardamom in small bowl until smooth. Chill until ready to serve. Makes 1/2 cup (125 mL) cream.

Soup: Put next 3 ingredients into large bowl. Drizzle with first amount of olive oil. Toss until coated. Spread evenly on ungreased baking sheet with sides. Bake in 425°F (220°C) oven for about 20 minutes until yam and carrot are tender-crisp. Cool. Transfer yam and garlic to cutting board. Discard yam and garlic peels. Chop yam. Set aside.

Heat second amount of olive oil in large saucepan on medium. Add leek and ginger. Cook for about 5 minutes, stirring occasionally, until leek is softened.

(continued on next page)

Add next 3 ingredients and roasted vegetables. Stir. Bring to a boil. Reduce heat to medium-low. Simmer, partially covered, for about 10 minutes, stirring occasionally, until vegetables are tender. Carefully process with hand blender or in blender until smooth (see Safety Tip).

Add cream. Heat and stir for about 2 minutes until heated through. Makes about 7 cups (1.75 L). Spoon Cardamom Cream on individual servings. Serves 6.

1 serving: 215 Calories; 8.7 g Total Fat (4.0 g Mono, 0.6 g Poly, 4.0 g Sat); 15 mg Cholesterol; 31 g Carbohydrate; 4 g Fibre; 5 g Protein; 854 mg Sodium

Safety Tip: Follow manufacturer's instructions for processing hot liquids.

Paré Pointer

When the chicken died…
They fed us roast chicken.
When the pig died…
They fed us roast pig.
When the farmer died…
We left in a hurry!

Creamy Kale Soup

*Not too thin, not too heavy, but loaded with flavour. Cream and
potatoes mellow the spicy bite of Mexican sausage and chili.*

Bacon slices, diced	2	2
Chorizo sausage, casing removed, chopped	8 oz.	225 g
Diced onion	1 cup	250 mL
Garlic cloves, minced (or 1/2 tsp., 2 mL, powder)	2	2
All-purpose flour	2 tsp.	10 mL
Chicken stock	6 cups	1.5 L
Dried crushed chilies	1/4 tsp.	1 mL
Medium unpeeled baking potatoes	2	2
Shredded kale leaves, lightly packed	1 cup	250 mL
Half-and-half cream	1 cup	250 mL
Grated Parmesan cheese, for garnish		

Cook bacon in large saucepan on medium until almost crisp. Add sausage.
Scramble-fry for about 5 minutes until sausage is browned. Transfer sausage
and bacon with slotted spoon to paper towel-lined plate to drain. Set aside.

Heat 2 tsp. (10 mL) drippings in same saucepan on medium. Add onion
and garlic. Cook for 5 to 10 minutes, stirring often, until onion is softened.

Sprinkle with flour. Heat and stir for 1 minute. Add stock and chilies. Stir.
Bring to a boil.

Cut potatoes in half lengthwise. Cut crosswise into 1/4 inch (6 mm)
slices, making half moons. Add to stock. Boil gently, partially covered,
for 10 minutes until potato is almost tender.

Add kale and sausage mixture. Boil gently, partially covered, for 5 minutes.
Remove from heat.

Add cream. Stir. Garnish individual servings with Parmesan cheese. Makes
about 9 cups (2.25 L).

*1 cup (250 mL): 289 Calories; 14.6 g Total Fat (6.2 g Mono, 1.2 g Poly, 6.4 g Sat);
3 mg Cholesterol; 15 g Carbohydrate; 1 g Fibre; 10 g Protein; 924 mg Sodium*

Pictured on page 72.

Creamy Pepper Tomato Soup

This smooth soup is a real pepper-upper!
Garnish with herbed croutons or chopped fresh basil.

Cooking oil	2 tsp.	10 mL
Chopped onion	1 cup	250 mL
Chopped celery	1/2 cup	125 mL
Chopped carrot	1/2 cup	125 mL
Garlic clove, minced (or 1/4 tsp., 1 mL, powder)	1	1
All-purpose flour	2 tbsp.	30 mL
Vegetable (or chicken) stock	3 cups	750 mL
Can of plum tomatoes (with juice)	14 oz.	398 mL
Jar of roasted red peppers, drained, blotted dry, chopped	14 oz.	398 mL
Tomato paste (see Tip, page 49)	1 tbsp.	15 mL
Dried rosemary, crushed	1/4 tsp.	1 mL
Bay leaf	1	1
Cream cheese, softened	1/4 cup	60 mL

Heat cooking oil in large saucepan on medium. Add next 4 ingredients. Cook for 5 to 10 minutes, stirring often, until onion is softened.

Sprinkle with flour. Heat and stir for 1 minute.

Add 1 cup (250 mL) stock. Heat and stir until boiling and thickened. Add remaining stock and next 5 ingredients. Stir. Bring to a boil. Reduce heat to medium-low. Simmer, covered, for 15 minutes, stirring occasionally, to blend flavours. Discard bay leaf.

Add cream cheese. Carefully process with hand blender or in blender until smooth (see Safety Tip). Makes about 7 cups (1.75 L).

1 cup (250 mL): 84 Calories; 3.6 g Total Fat (1.3 g Mono, 0.6 g Poly, 1.3 g Sat); 6 mg Cholesterol; 11 g Carbohydrate; 2 g Fibre; 3 g Protein; 600 mg Sodium

Pictured on page 107.

Safety Tip: Follow manufacturer's instructions for processing hot liquids.

Roasted Garlic Potato Soup

Almonds and roasted garlic add flavour and texture to this unusual soup.
Your family will be nutty about it. Factor in extra time to roast the garlic.

Garlic bulbs	3	3
Cooking oil	1 tbsp.	15 mL
Chopped onion	1 cup	250 mL
Diced peeled potato	2 cups	500 mL
Salt	1/4 tsp.	1 mL
Dry (or alcohol-free) white wine	1/3 cup	75 mL
Chicken (or vegetable) stock	4 cups	1 L
Bay leaf	1	1
Dried thyme	1/4 tsp.	1 mL
Pepper	1/4 tsp.	1 mL
Slivered almonds, toasted (see Tip, page 83)	1/2 cup	125 mL
Milk	3/4 cup	175 mL
Chopped fresh parsley	1/4 cup	60 mL

Trim 1/4 inch (6 mm) from garlic bulbs to expose tops of cloves, leaving bulbs intact. Wrap loosely in greased foil. Bake in 375°F (190°C) oven for about 45 minutes until tender. Let stand until cool enough to handle. Squeeze garlic bulbs to remove cloves from peel. Discard peel. Set aside.

Heat cooking oil in large saucepan on medium. Add onion. Cook for 5 to 10 minutes until softened.

Add potato and salt. Stir. Add wine. Cook and stir on medium-high for about 2 minutes until wine is almost evaporated.

Add next 4 ingredients. Stir. Bring to a boil. Reduce heat to medium-low. Simmer, covered, for 10 minutes. Add roasted garlic. Simmer, covered, for 5 to 10 minutes until potato is tender. Transfer to large bowl. Cool slightly. Discard bay leaf. Carefully transfer 2 cups (500 mL) soup to blender or food processor.

Add almonds to blender. Process until smooth (see Safety Tip). Return to same saucepan. Process remaining soup in blender or food processor until smooth. Return to saucepan.

Add milk and parsley. Heat and stir on medium for 2 to 3 minutes until heated through. Makes about 7 cups (1.75 L).

(continued on next page)

1 cup (250 mL): 173 Calories; 7.9 g Total Fat (4.6 g Mono, 1.8 g Poly, 1.1 g Sat); 1 mg Cholesterol; 20 g Carbohydrate; 3 g Fibre; 6 g Protein; 598 mg Sodium

Safety Tip: Follow manufacturer's instructions for processing hot liquids.

Stilton Cauliflower Soup

Say cheese! Blue cheese lovers will be in raptures over this velvety purée.

Small head of cauliflower (about 1 lb., 454 g), cut into small florets	1	1
Butter (or hard margarine)	2 tbsp.	30 mL
Chopped onion	1 1/2 cups	375 mL
Chopped celery	1 cup	250 mL
Bay leaf	1	1
Ground sage	1/4 tsp.	1 mL
Salt	1/4 tsp.	1 mL
Pepper	1/4 tsp.	1 mL
All-purpose flour	1/4 cup	60 mL
Vegetable stock	4 cups	1 L
Milk	1 cup	250 mL
Crumbled Stilton (or other blue) cheese	1/4 cup	60 mL

Cook 1 cup (250 mL) of cauliflower florets in boiling salted water in small saucepan for about 2 minutes until tender-crisp. Drain. Plunge into ice water in medium bowl. Let stand for 10 minutes until cold. Drain. Set aside.

Melt butter in large saucepan on medium. Add next 6 ingredients and remaining cauliflower. Stir. Cook, covered, for about 10 minutes, stirring occasionally, until onion is softened.

Sprinkle with flour. Heat and stir for 1 minute. Slowly add 2 cups (500 mL) stock. Heat and stir until boiling and thickened. Add milk and remaining stock. Stir. Bring to a boil. Reduce heat to medium-low. Simmer, partially covered, for about 15 minutes, stirring occasionally, until cauliflower is tender. Discard bay leaf. Carefully process with hand blender or in blender until smooth (see Safety Tip).

Add cheese and reserved cauliflower florets. Heat and stir until heated through. Makes about 7 cups (1.75 L).

1 cup (250 mL): 113 Calories; 5.7 g Total Fat (1.5 g Mono, 0.3 g Poly, 3.6 g Sat); 14 mg Cholesterol; 12 g Carbohydrate; 1 g Fibre; 5 g Protein; 724 mg Sodium

Safety Tip: Follow manufacturer's instructions for processing hot liquids.

Crab Asparagus Soup

This velvety-green soup is so good, it's almost sinful. But don't worry, your nearest and dearest will think you're an absolute angel every time you make it.

Fresh asparagus (see Note)	2 lbs.	900 g
Butter (or hard margarine)	2 tbsp.	30 mL
Sliced leek (white part only)	1 cup	250 mL
Garlic cloves, minced (or 1/4 tsp., 1 mL, powder)	1	1
Ground nutmeg	1/8 tsp.	0.5 mL
All-purpose flour	2 tbsp.	30 mL
Chicken stock	5 cups	1.25 L
Can of crabmeat, drained, cartilage removed, flaked	5 oz.	142 g
Whipping cream	1/2 cup	125 mL
Salt	1/4 tsp.	1 mL
Pepper	1/4 tsp.	1 mL

Cut 1 inch (2.5 cm) tips off of asparagus stalks. Cook tips in boiling water in small saucepan for about 2 minutes until bright green. Drain. Plunge into ice water in small bowl. Let stand for 5 minutes until cold. Drain. Set aside. Chop remaining stalks.

Melt butter in large saucepan on medium. Add next 3 ingredients and asparagus stalks. Cook for about 10 minutes, stirring occasionally, until asparagus starts to soften.

Sprinkle with flour. Heat and stir for 1 minute. Slowly add 1 cup (250 mL) stock. Heat and stir until boiling and thickened. Add remaining stock. Stir. Bring to a boil. Reduce heat to medium-low. Simmer, partially covered, for about 10 minutes until asparagus is tender. Carefully process in blender until almost smooth (see Safety Tip). Press through sieve into separate large saucepan. Discard solids.

Add remaining 4 ingredients. Stir. Slice asparagus tips. Add to soup. Heat and stir on medium for about 5 minutes until heated through. Makes about 7 cups (1.75 L).

1 cup (250 mL): 159 Calories; 10.0 g Total Fat (2.7 g Mono, 0.5 g Poly, 6.1 g Sat); 30 mg Cholesterol; 12 g Carbohydrate; 3 g Fibre; 8 g Protein; 876 mg Sodium

Pictured on page 90 and on back cover.

Safety Tip: Follow manufacturer's instructions for processing hot liquids.

Note: No need to remove the tough ends of the asparagus as the soup will be blended.

Cream Of Mushroom Soup

A delightfully creamy mushroom and dill soup—perked up with a little paprika.

Butter (or hard margarine)	2 tbsp.	30 mL
Thinly sliced fresh brown (or white) mushrooms (about 1 1/2 lbs., 680 g)	10 cups	2.5 L
Butter (or hard margarine)	1 tbsp.	15 mL
Finely chopped onion	2 1/2 cups	625 mL
Chopped fresh dill (or 1 tbsp., 15 mL, dill weed)	1/4 cup	60 mL
Paprika	2 tsp.	10 mL
Salt	1/2 tsp.	2 mL
Pepper	1/4 tsp.	1 mL
All-purpose flour	1/4 cup	60 mL
Chicken (or vegetable) stock	3 cups	750 mL
Dry (or alcohol-free) white wine	1/2 cup	125 mL
Half-and-half cream	1 cup	250 mL
Chopped fresh parsley	3 tbsp.	50 mL
Sour cream	1/4 cup	60 mL
Lemon juice	1 1/2 tbsp.	25 mL

Melt first amount of butter in large saucepan on medium-high. Add mushrooms. Cook for about 10 minutes, stirring often, until mushrooms are browned and liquid is evaporated.

Add next 6 ingredients. Cook and stir on medium until second amount of butter is melted. Cook, covered, for 5 to 10 minutes, stirring occasionally, until onion is softened.

Sprinkle with flour. Heat and stir for 1 minute. Slowly add 2 cups (500 mL) stock. Heat and stir until boiling and thickened. Add wine and remaining stock. Stir. Bring to a boil. Reduce heat to medium-low. Simmer, covered, for 15 minutes, stirring occasionally, to blend flavours.

Add cream and parsley. Stir.

Combine sour cream and lemon juice in small cup. Drizzle onto individual servings. Makes about 7 cups (1.75 L).

1 cup (250 mL): 188 Calories; 10.7 g Total Fat (2.9 g Mono, 0.6 g Poly, 6.5 g Sat); 28 mg Cholesterol; 17 g Carbohydrate; 3 g Fibre; 6 g Protein; 615 mg Sodium

Pictured on page 89.

Pastry-Topped Mushroom Soup

Don't keep this marvelous mushroom creation in the dark!
We've paired this creamy soup with a decadent pastry top,
but it's also excellent served on its own.

Fresh whole white mushrooms	1 1/4 lbs.	560 g
Butter (or hard margarine)	2 tsp.	10 mL
Chopped onion	3/4 cup	175 mL
Butter (or hard margarine)	2 tsp.	10 mL
Medium sherry	3 tbsp.	50 mL
Butter (or hard margarine)	1/4 cup	60 mL
All-purpose flour	1/4 cup	60 mL
Chicken stock	4 cups	1 L
Bay leaf	1	1
Ground thyme	1/2 tsp.	2 mL
Salt	1/4 tsp.	1 mL
Pepper	1/2 tsp.	2 mL
Half-and-half cream	1/2 cup	125 mL
Medium sherry	2 tbsp.	30 mL
Package of puff pastry (14 oz., 397 g), thawed according to package directions	1/2	1/2
Large egg, fork-beaten	1	1

Separate mushroom caps and stems. Slice enough mushroom caps to make 2 cups (500 mL). Set aside. Chop remaining caps and stems.

Heat first amount of butter in large saucepan on medium-high. Add onion and chopped mushrooms. Cook for about 5 minutes, stirring often, until mushrooms release liquid. Transfer to medium bowl. Set aside.

Heat second amount of butter in same saucepan on medium. Add reserved sliced mushrooms. Cook for about 10 minutes, stirring often, until liquid is evaporated.

Add first amount of sherry. Heat and stir for 1 minute. Transfer to small bowl. Set aside.

(continued on next page)

Heat third amount of butter in same saucepan until melted. Add flour. Stir constantly for about 1 minute until mixture comes together to make a roux (see Thickening Tricks, page 9).

Slowly add 2 cups (500 mL) stock, stirring constantly with a whisk, until boiling and slightly thickened. Add remaining stock and next 4 ingredients. Stir. Add onion mixture. Reduce heat to medium-low. Simmer, partially covered, for 10 minutes to blend flavours. Discard bay leaf. Carefully process with hand blender or in blender until smooth.

Add cream, second amount of sherry and mushroom mixture. Heat and stir until heated through. Makes about 6 cups (1.5 L). Ladle soup into six 1 cup (250 mL) ovenproof ramekins. Place on baking sheet with sides. Set aside.

Roll out puff pastry on lightly floured surface to 10 × 15 inch (25 cm × 37 cm) rectangle. Cut into six 5 inch (12.5 cm) squares (see Note).

Brush top rim of ramekins with egg. Place 1 pastry square over each ramekin. Press pastry to ramekins to seal. Gently brush egg on pastry. Bake in 400°F (205°C) oven for about 20 minutes until pastry is puffed and golden. Serves 6.

1 serving: 387 Calories; 27.2 g Total Fat (6.9 g Mono, 8.1 g Poly, 10.5 g Sat); 72 mg Cholesterol; 28 g Carbohydrate; 2 g Fibre; 8 g Protein; 888 mg Sodium

Note: For easy rolling, puff pastry should be cool. Always wrap pastry in plastic wrap if not using immediately.

Paré Pointer
Did the jelly roll because it saw the apple turn over?

Roasted Garlic Fennel Soup

Jack was probably thinking of this soup when he sold his cow for a handful of beans. Who needs meat when garlic and fennel are providing so much flavour?

Garlic bulbs	2	2
Olive (or cooking) oil	2 tsp.	10 mL
Chopped fennel bulb (white part only)	2 cups	500 mL
Chopped onion	1 cup	250 mL
Celery rib, with leaves, sliced	1	1
Chicken (or vegetable) stock	4 1/2 cups	1.1 L
Can of white kidney beans, rinsed and drained	19 oz.	540 mL
Dried rosemary, crushed	1/4 tsp.	1 mL

Trim 1/4 inch (6 mm) from garlic bulbs to expose tops of cloves, leaving bulbs intact. Wrap loosely in greased foil. Bake in 375°F (190°C) oven for about 45 minutes until softened. Let stand until cool enough to handle. Squeeze garlic bulbs to remove cloves from peel. Discard peel. Place cloves in small bowl. Set aside.

Heat olive oil in large saucepan on medium. Add next 3 ingredients. Cook for about 10 minutes, stirring often, until onion is softened.

Add roasted garlic and remaining 3 ingredients. Stir. Bring to a boil. Reduce heat to medium-low. Simmer, covered, for about 20 minutes, stirring occasionally, until fennel is tender. Carefully process with hand blender or in blender until smooth (see Safety Tip). Makes about 7 cups (1.75 L). ·

1 cup (250 mL): 88 Calories; 1.9 g Total Fat (1.0 g Mono, 0.2 g Poly, 0.5 g Sat); 0 mg Cholesterol; 14 g Carbohydrate; 3 g Fibre; 5 g Protein; 658 mg Sodium

Pictured at right.

Safety Tip: Follow manufacturer's instructions for processing hot liquids.

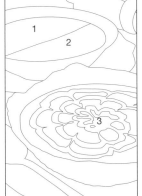

1. Creamy Pepper Tomato Soup, page 99
2. Roasted Garlic Fennel Soup, above
3. Melon Berry Soup, page 43

Props courtesy of: Cherison Enterprises Inc.
Pfaltzgraff Canada

Mellow Yellow Soup

Who wouldn't be mellow after supping on this sunny, golden split-pea soup?

Cooking oil	2 tsp.	10 mL
Chopped onion	1 cup	250 mL
Grated carrot	1 cup	250 mL
Vegetable (or chicken) stock	6 cups	1.5 L
Chopped yellow zucchini (with peel), (see Note)	1 1/2 cups	375 mL
Chopped, peeled sweet potato (or yam)	1 cup	250 mL
Frozen kernel corn	1 cup	250 mL
Yellow split peas, rinsed and drained	3/4 cup	175 mL
Dill weed	1/2 tsp.	2 mL
Turmeric	1/4 tsp.	1 mL
Dried thyme	1/4 tsp.	1 mL
Bay leaf	1	1

Heat cooking oil in large saucepan on medium. Add onion and carrot. Cook for 5 to 10 minutes, stirring often, until onion is softened.

Add remaining 9 ingredients. Stir. Bring to a boil. Reduce heat to medium-low. Simmer, covered, for about 1 hour, stirring occasionally, until sweet potato is tender and split peas are very soft. Discard bay leaf. Makes about 8 cups (2 L).

1 cup (250 mL): 101 Calories; 1.9 g Total Fat (0.8 g Mono, 0.5 g Poly, 0.5 g Sat); 0 mg Cholesterol; 18 g Carbohydrate; 3 g Fibre; 5 g Protein; 700 mg Sodium

Pictured at left.

Note: If yellow zucchini is not available, use peeled green zucchini.

1. Moroccan Lentil Soup, page 111
2. Mellow Yellow Soup, above

Props courtesy of: Danesco Inc.

Lemon Lentil Soup

Vibrant Mediterranean flavours with a fresh lemon background will have you tasting a whole new spectrum of delights.

Olive (or cooking) oil	1 tbsp.	15 mL
Diced onion	1 1/2 cups	375 mL
Diced carrot	1 cup	250 mL
Chopped fresh oregano (or 1 1/4 tsp., 6 mL, dried)	1 1/2 tbsp.	25 mL
Garlic cloves, minced	3	3
Chopped fresh rosemary (or 1/4 tsp., 1 mL, dried, crushed)	1 tsp.	5 mL
Salt	1/2 tsp.	2 mL
Pepper	1/2 tsp.	2 mL
Dried crushed chilies	1/4 tsp.	1 mL
Bay leaf	1	1
Chicken stock	6 cups	1.5 L
Dried red split lentils	1 1/2 cups	375 mL
Lemon juice	6 tbsp.	100 mL
Grated lemon zest	1 tsp.	5 mL
Pepper	1/8 tsp.	0.5 mL
Crumbled feta cheese	1/4 cup	60 mL
Chopped fresh parsley	1/4 cup	60 mL

Heat olive oil in large saucepan on medium-high. Add onion. Cook for 5 to 10 minutes, stirring often, until onion starts to brown.

Add next 8 ingredients. Cook for about 3 minutes, stirring often, until carrot is tender-crisp.

Add chicken stock and lentils. Bring to a boil. Reduce heat to medium-low. Simmer, partially covered, for about 20 minutes, stirring occasionally, until lentils are very soft. Discard bay leaf.

Stir in next 3 ingredients.

Sprinkle feta cheese and parsley on individual servings. Makes about 7 cups (1.75 L).

1 cup (250 mL): 228 Calories; 4.3 g Total Fat (1.8 g Mono, 0.5 g Poly, 1.7 g Sat); 5 mg Cholesterol; 35 g Carbohydrate; 6 g Fibre; 15 g Protein; 995 mg Sodium

Pictured on page 126.

Healthful Legumes

Moroccan Lentil Soup

You'll rock the casbah with this Moroccan-inspired delight. The exotic spices in this vegetarian soup add flavour and a comforting aroma to soft lentils.

Cooking oil	2 tsp.	10 mL
Chopped onion	1 cup	250 mL
Finely grated ginger root	2 tsp.	10 mL
Garlic cloves, minced	2	2
Ground turmeric	1 tsp.	5 mL
Ground cumin	1 tsp.	5 mL
Ground cinnamon	1 tsp.	5 mL
Bay leaf	1	1
Salt	1/8 tsp.	0.5 mL
Vegetable (or chicken) stock	6 cups	1.5 L
Dried green lentils	1 cup	250 mL
Diced carrot	1 cup	250 mL
Diced celery	1/2 cup	125 mL
Lemon juice	1 tbsp.	15 mL
Chopped fresh cilantro or parsley	1 tbsp.	15 mL
Grated lemon zest	1 tsp.	5 mL

Heat cooking oil in large saucepan on medium. Add onion. Cook for 5 to 10 minutes, stirring often, until softened.

Add next 7 ingredients. Heat and stir for about 1 minute until fragrant.

Add next 4 ingredients. Bring to a boil. Reduce heat to medium-low. Simmer, partially covered, for about 1 hour, stirring occasionally, until lentils are very soft. Discard bay leaf.

Add remaining 3 ingredients. Stir. Makes about 7 cups (1.75 L).

1 cup (250 mL): 151 Calories; 2.2 g Total Fat (0.8 g Mono, 0.6 g Poly, 0.6 g Sat); 0 mg Cholesterol; 24 g Carbohydrate; 4 g Fibre; 10 g Protein; 808 mg Sodium

Pictured on page 108.

Beef Lentil Vegetable Soup

To spice or not to spice? We've added hot sauce to this brothy soup,
but you can go as hot, or not, as you like. Serve with whole wheat buns.

Cooking oil	1 tbsp.	15 mL
Stewing beef, cut into 1/2 inch (12 mm) pieces	3/4 lb.	340 g
Beef stock	8 cups	2 L
Chopped onion	1 1/2 cups	375 mL
Chopped carrot	1 1/2 cups	375 mL
Chopped yellow turnip	1 1/2 cups	375 mL
Chopped celery	1 cup	250 mL
Worcestershire sauce	2 tbsp.	30 mL
Chopped fresh thyme (or 3/4 tsp., 4 mL, dried)	1 tbsp.	15 mL
Hot pepper sauce	1 tsp.	5 mL
Pepper	1/2 tsp.	2 mL
Can of lentils, rinsed and drained	19 oz.	540 mL

Heat cooking oil in Dutch oven or large pot on medium-high. Add beef. Cook for 5 to 10 minutes, stirring occasionally, until browned.

Add next 9 ingredients. Stir. Bring to a boil. Reduce heat to medium-low. Simmer, covered, for about 45 minutes, stirring occasionally, until beef is tender.

Add lentils. Stir. Cook, covered, for about 10 minutes, stirring occasionally, until lentils are heated through. Makes about 13 cups (3.25 L).

1 cup (250 mL): 113 Calories; 3.5 g Total Fat (1.6 g Mono, 0.5 g Poly, 1.0 g Sat); 14 mg Cholesterol; 10 g Carbohydrate; 2 g Fibre; 10 g Protein; 656 mg Sodium

Paré Pointer
Our photographer uses burned out light bulbs in his darkroom.

White Bean And Spinach Soup

You're strong to the finish, 'cause you eat your spinach—and beans. Pop this protein-laden soup in your slow cooker when you need a little energy.

Cooking oil	1 tsp.	5 mL
Lean ground chicken	1 lb.	454 g
Chopped onion	1 cup	250 mL
Diced carrot	1 cup	250 mL
Garlic cloves, minced (or 1/2 tsp., 2 mL, powder)	2	2
Ground cumin	1/2 tsp.	2 mL
Chicken stock	5 cups	1.25 L
Can of black-eyed beans, rinsed and drained	19 oz.	540 mL
Can of navy beans, rinsed and drained	14 oz.	398 mL
Grated lemon zest	1 tsp.	5 mL
Fresh spinach leaves, lightly packed	3 cups	750 mL
Lemon juice	1 tbsp.	15 mL
Salt	1/4 tsp.	1 mL

Heat cooking oil in large frying pan on medium. Add chicken. Scramble-fry for about 10 minutes until no longer pink.

Add next 4 ingredients. Cook for 5 to 10 minutes, stirring occasionally, until onion is softened. Transfer to 4 to 5 quart (4 to 5 L) slow cooker.

Add next 4 ingredients. Stir. Cook, covered, on Low for 6 hours or on High for 3 hours until carrot is tender.

Add spinach. Stir well. Cook, covered, on High for about 5 minutes until spinach is wilted.

Add lemon juice and salt. Stir. Makes about 10 cups (2.5 L).

1 cup (250 mL): 182 Calories; 7.2 g Total Fat (0.3 g Mono, 0.3 g Poly, 0.4 g Sat); 0 mg Cholesterol; 16 g Carbohydrate; 4 g Fibre; 14 g Protein; 656 mg Sodium

Country Bean Soup

*You and your country cousin can pop this high-protein treat in a slow cooker,
sit back and watch the corn grow. Serve with crusty rolls. Delicious.*

Dried navy beans	1 1/2 cups	375 mL
Chicken stock	7 cups	1.75 L
Chopped carrot	1 cup	250 mL
Chopped onion	1 cup	250 mL
Garlic cloves, minced (or 1/2 tsp., 2 mL, powder)	2	2
Chopped fresh thyme (or 1/2 tsp., 2 mL, dried)	2 tsp.	10 mL
Chopped fresh rosemary (or 1/2 tsp., 2 mL, dried, crushed)	2 tsp.	10 mL
Bay leaf	1	1
Cooking oil	2 tsp.	10 mL
Bone-in chicken thighs, skin removed	1 lb.	454 g
Sliced smoked ham sausage (about 3/4 lb., 340 g)	2 cups	500 mL
Tomato paste (see Tip, page 49)	1/4 cup	60 mL
Chopped fresh parsley	1/4 cup	60 mL

Measure beans into medium heatproof bowl. Add boiling water until
2 inches (5 cm) above beans. Let stand for at least 1 hour until cool. Drain.
Rinse beans. Drain. Transfer to 5 to 7 quart (5 to 7 L) slow cooker.

Add next 7 ingredients. Stir.

Heat cooking oil in medium frying pan on medium-high. Add chicken. Cook
for about 2 minutes per side until browned. Add to slow cooker. Cook,
covered, on Low for 9 to 10 hours or on High for 4 1/2 to 5 hours. Discard
bay leaf. Remove chicken to cutting board using slotted spoon. Remove
chicken from bones. Discard bones. Add chicken to slow cooker.

Add ham sausage and tomato paste. Stir well. Cook, covered, on High for
about 15 minutes until heated through.

Add parsley. Stir. Makes about 12 cups (3 L).

*1 cup (250 mL): 209 Calories; 6.0 g Total Fat (0.9 g Mono, 0.7 g Poly, 0.8 g Sat); 19 mg Cholesterol;
23 g Carbohydrate; 5 g Fibre; 17 g Protein; 788 mg Sodium*

Greek Minestrone

*Opa! We've taken this traditionally Italian dish and Greeked it up.
The fabulous flavours of salty olives and feta will have you throwing
plates in no time (as is the custom in some Greek restaurants).*

Olive (or cooking) oil	2 tsp.	10 mL
Chopped onion	1 cup	250 mL
Fennel bulb (white part only), chopped	1 cup	250 mL
Garlic cloves, minced (or 1/2 tsp., 2 mL, powder)	2	2
Chopped zucchini (with peel)	1 cup	250 mL
Chopped eggplant (with peel)	1 cup	250 mL
Diced red pepper	1 cup	250 mL
Chicken (or vegetable) stock	4 cups	1 L
Can of chickpeas (garbanzo beans), rinsed and drained	19 oz.	540 mL
Can of plum tomatoes (with juice), chopped	14 oz.	398 mL
Bay leaf	1	1
Dried oregano	1/2 tsp.	2 mL
Dried thyme	1/2 tsp.	2 mL
Pepper	1/4 tsp.	1 mL
Can of sliced black olives, drained	4 1/2 oz.	125 mL
Chopped fresh basil	3 tbsp.	50 mL
Crumbled feta cheese	1/2 cup	125 mL

Heat olive oil in large saucepan on medium. Add next 3 ingredients. Cook for about 5 minutes, stirring often, until onion is softened.

Add next 3 ingredients. Cook for about 3 minutes, stirring occasionally, until red pepper starts to soften.

Add next 7 ingredients. Bring to a boil. Reduce heat to medium-low. Simmer, partially covered, for about 15 minutes, stirring occasionally, until vegetables are very soft. Discard bay leaf.

Add olives and basil. Stir.

Sprinkle feta cheese on individual servings. Makes about 9 cups (2.25 L).

1 cup (250 mL): 119 Calories; 4.6 g Total Fat (1.7 g Mono, 0.6 g Poly, 1.9 g Sat); 8 mg Cholesterol; 15 g Carbohydrate; 3 g Fibre; 6 g Protein; 670 mg Sodium

Black Bean Soup

*This high-in-fibre soup is about the tastiest way you can add
fibre into your diet. A swirl of sour cream and a sprinkle of
green onion easily enhance its southwestern flavour.*

Dried black beans	2 cups	500 mL
Bacon slices, diced	6	6
Chopped onion	1 cup	250 mL
Chopped carrot	3/4 cup	175 mL
Chopped celery	3/4 cup	175 mL
Garlic cloves, minced	3	3
Bay leaves	2	2
Ground cumin	1 tsp.	5 mL
Chili powder	1/2 tsp.	2 mL
Ground coriander	1/2 tsp.	2 mL
Dried oregano	1/2 tsp.	2 mL
Pepper	1/2 tsp.	2 mL
Cayenne pepper	1/4 tsp.	1 mL
Chicken stock	6 cups	1.5 L
Chili sauce	1/2 cup	125 mL

Sour cream, for garnish
Sliced green onion, for garnish

Measure beans into medium heatproof bowl. Add boiling water until
2 inches (5 cm) above beans. Cover. Let stand for at least 1 hour until
cool. Drain. Rinse beans. Drain. Set aside.

Cook bacon in large saucepan on medium until crisp.

Add next 4 ingredients. Cook for 5 to 10 minutes, stirring often, until
onion is softened.

Add next 7 ingredients. Heat and stir for about 1 minute until fragrant.

Add stock, chili sauce and beans. Bring to a boil. Reduce heat to
medium-low. Simmer, partially covered, for about 2 hours, stirring
occasionally, until beans are tender. Discard bay leaves. Carefully process
with hand blender or in blender until smooth (see Safety Tip).

(continued on next page)

Garnish individual servings with sour cream and green onion. Makes about 8 cups (2 L).

1 cup (250 mL): 306 Calories; 9.3 g Total Fat (5.8 g Mono, 1.8 g Poly, 5.2 g Sat); 12 mg Cholesterol; 42 g Carbohydrate; 9 g Fibre; 15 g Protein; 1022 mg Sodium

Safety Tip: Follow manufacturer's instructions for processing hot liquids.

WHITE BEAN SOUP: Omit black beans. Use same amount of dried white kidney beans. Cook as directed.

RED BEAN SOUP: Omit black beans. Use same amount of dried pinto (or other red) beans. Cook as directed.

Paré Pointer

Our landlord believed in the hereafter.
He kept coming here after the rent.

Lamb Bouquet Soup

Savvy shepherds know a soup made in a slow cooker is all the better.

Dried navy beans	1 cup	250 mL
Beef (or chicken) stock	7 cups	1.75 L
Lamb shanks (about 1 1/2 lbs., 680 g)	2	2
Chopped onion	1 cup	250 mL
Chopped celery	1 cup	250 mL
Pot barley	1/2 cup	125 mL
Sliced carrot	1/2 cup	125 mL
Chopped fresh rosemary (or 1/2 tsp., 2 mL, dried, crushed)	2 tsp.	10 mL
Paprika	1/2 tsp.	2 mL
ALLSPICE BOUQUET GARNI		
Bay leaves	2	2
Whole allspice	2	2
Fresh parsley sprigs	2	2
Whole black peppercorns	8	8
Garlic clove	1	1
Diced fresh tomato	1 1/2 cups	375 mL
Brown sugar, packed	2 tbsp.	30 mL
Grated lemon zest	1 tsp.	5 mL
Salt	1/2 tsp.	2 mL

Measure beans into small heatproof bowl. Add boiling water until 2 inches (5 cm) above beans. Let stand for at least 1 hour until cool. Drain. Rinse beans. Drain. Transfer to 5 to 7 quart (5 to 7 L) slow cooker.

Add next 8 ingredients. Stir.

Allspice Bouquet Garni: Place first 5 ingredients on 10 inch (25 cm) square piece of cheesecloth. Draw up corners and tie with butcher's string. Submerge in liquid in slow cooker. Cook, covered, on Low for about 10 hours or on High for about 5 hours until beans are tender and lamb is falling off bones. Remove and discard bouquet garni. Remove shanks to cutting board using slotted spoon. Keep bean mixture covered. Remove lamb from bones. Discard bones. Chop lamb coarsely. Return to slow cooker.

Add remaining 4 ingredients. Stir. Cook, covered, on High for about 15 minutes until heated through. Makes about 12 cups (3 L).

(continued on next page)

1 cup (250 mL): 247 Calories; 10.4 g Total Fat (4.1 g Mono, 1.0 g Poly, 4.4 g Sat); 33 mg Cholesterol; 23 g Carbohydrate; 5 g Fibre; 15 g Protein; 639 mg Sodium

---

Curried Chickpea Soup

On the table in 30 minutes or less! Garnish with chopped mango chutney.

Cooking oil	2 tbsp.	30 mL
Finely chopped onion	1 1/2 cups	375 mL
Finely chopped, peeled and seeded English cucumber	1 cup	250 mL
Finely chopped, peeled cooking apple (such as McIntosh)	1 cup	250 mL
Finely grated gingerroot	4 tsp.	20 mL
Garlic cloves, minced	3	3
Bay leaf	1	1
Curry powder	1 tsp.	5 mL
Ground cumin	1/2 tsp.	2 mL
Ground coriander	1/2 tsp.	2 mL
Paprika	1/2 tsp.	2 mL
Salt	1/2 tsp.	2 mL
Chicken stock	6 cups	1.5 L
Can of chickpeas (garbanzo beans), rinsed and drained	19 oz.	540 mL
Can of tomato sauce	7 1/2 oz.	213 mL
Can of coconut milk	14 oz.	398 mL
Sweet chili sauce	2 tbsp.	30 mL

Heat cooking oil in Dutch oven or large pot on medium. Add onion. Cook for 5 to 10 minutes, stirring often, until softened.

Add next 10 ingredients. Heat and stir for about 3 minutes until fragrant.

Add next 3 ingredients. Stir. Bring to a boil. Reduce heat to medium-low. Simmer, uncovered, for 10 minutes to blend flavours.

Add coconut milk and chili sauce. Heat and stir until heated through. Discard bay leaf. Carefully process with hand blender or in blender until smooth (see Safety Tip). Makes about 11 cups (2.75 L).

1 cup (250 mL): 163 Calories; 10.9 g Total Fat (2.0 g Mono, 1.1 g Poly, 7.1 g Sat); 0 mg Cholesterol; 14 g Carbohydrate; 2 g Fibre; 4 g Protein; 797 mg Sodium

Safety Tip: Follow manufacturer's instructions for processing hot liquids.

Peanut Yam Soup

Think yams are yum? Then this is the soup for you!
Roasted garlic and yam become exotic when combined with peanuts,
cumin and coriander. Roasting vegetables is a great way to add flavour
to dishes without adding extra fat. As vegetables roast, the natural sugars
caramelize. Factor in extra time to roast the garlic and yams.

Garlic bulb	1	1
Small unpeeled yams (or sweet potatoes) (about 2 1/2 lbs., 1.1 kg)	4	4
Unsalted roasted peanuts	3/4 cup	175 mL
Cooking oil	1 tbsp.	15 mL
Chopped onion	1 1/2 cups	375 mL
Ground cumin	1 tsp.	5 mL
Ground coriander	1 tsp.	5 mL
Salt	1/2 tsp.	2 mL
Pepper	1/4 tsp.	1 mL
Cayenne pepper	1/4 tsp.	1 mL
Chicken stock	6 cups	1.5 L
Can of diced tomatoes (with juice)	14 oz.	398 mL
Can of chickpeas (garbanzo beans), rinsed and drained	14 oz.	398 mL

Trim 1/4 inch (6 mm) from garlic bulb to expose tops of cloves, leaving bulb intact. Wrap loosely in greased foil. Place on ungreased baking sheet. Place yams on same baking sheet. Bake in 375°F (190°C) oven for about 45 minutes until garlic and yams are tender. Let stand until cool enough to handle. Squeeze garlic bulb to remove cloves from peel. Discard peel. Place cloves in medium bowl. Cut yams in half. Scoop yam from peel into same medium bowl. Discard peel.

Process peanuts in blender or food processor until very finely chopped. Add to yam mixture. Mash with fork. Set aside.

Heat cooking oil in Dutch oven or large pot on medium. Add onion. Cook, for 5 to 10 minutes, stirring often, until softened.

(continued on next page)

Add next 5 ingredients. Stir. Cook for about 5 minutes, stirring often, until onion is golden.

Add yam mixture and remaining 3 ingredients. Stir. Bring to a boil. Reduce heat to medium-low. Simmer, partially covered, for 15 minutes, stirring occasionally, to blend flavours. Carefully process with hand blender or in blender until smooth (see Safety Tip). Makes 12 cups (3 L).

1 cup (250 mL): 210 Calories; 7.0 g Total Fat (3.2 g Mono, 2.2 g Poly, 1.1 g Sat); 0 mg Cholesterol; 33 g Carbohydrate; 5 g Fibre; 7 g Protein; 634 mg Sodium

Safety Tip: Follow manufacturer's instructions for processing hot liquids.

Paré Pointer
The most dedicated dog we have is the
hot dog. It feeds the hand that bites it.

Mexican Pinto Bean Soup

A swirl of Jalapeño Lime Yogurt is a fitting topper for this spicy bean and rice soup. For a milder version, use less chili powder and a less-spicy sausage.

Cooking oil	1 tbsp.	15 mL
Chorizo sausage, casing removed, chopped	1	1
Chopped onion	3/4 cup	175 mL
Diced green pepper	3/4 cup	175 mL
Diced carrot	1/2 cup	125 mL
Garlic clove, minced (or 1/4 tsp., 1 mL, powder)	1	1
Pepper	1/4 tsp.	1 mL
Can of pinto (or romano) beans, rinsed and drained	19 oz.	540 mL
Chicken stock	5 cups	1.25 L
Can of diced tomatoes (with juice)	14 oz.	398 mL
Long grain white rice	1/2 cup	125 mL
Chunky salsa	1/2 cup	125 mL
Chili powder	2 tsp.	10 mL
Bay leaf	1	1
Dried oregano	1 tsp.	5 mL
Ground cinnamon	1/2 tsp.	2 mL

JALAPEÑO LIME YOGURT		
Plain yogurt	1/2 cup	125 mL
Sliced pickled jalapeño peppers, chopped	2 tbsp.	30 mL
Grated lime zest	1 tsp.	5 mL

Heat cooking oil in Dutch oven or large pot on medium. Add next 6 ingredients. Cook for 5 to 10 minutes, stirring occasionally, until onion is softened. Drain.

Mash half of pinto beans with fork on plate. Add to vegetable mixture.

Add next 8 ingredients and remaining pinto beans. Stir. Bring to a boil. Reduce heat to medium-low. Simmer, covered, for about 20 minutes, stirring occasionally, until rice is tender. Discard bay leaf. Makes about 11 cups (2.75 L).

(continued on next page)

Jalapeño Lime Yogurt: Combine all 3 ingredients in small cup. Makes about 2/3 cup (150 mL) yogurt. Drizzle onto individual servings. Serves 8.

1 serving: 285 Calories; 13.8 g Total Fat (6.4 g Mono, 1.7 g Poly, 4.8 g Sat); 26 mg Cholesterol; 28 g Carbohydrate; 5 g Fibre; 13 g Protein; 1113 mg Sodium

VEGETARIAN PINTO BEAN SOUP: Omit sausage and use vegetable stock instead of chicken stock.

___

Tex-Mex Taco Soup

This slow cooker soup is a fiesta of flavour!
Garnish individual servings with crushed taco chips.

Cooking Oil	2 tsp.	10 mL
Lean ground beef	1 lb.	454 g
Beef stock	6 cups	1.5 L
Can of kidney beans, rinsed and drained	19 oz.	540 mL
Chopped red onion	2 cups	500 mL
Can of diced tomatoes (with juice)	14 oz.	398 mL
Chopped celery	1 1/2 cups	375 mL
Grated carrot	1 1/2 cups	375 mL
Chopped green pepper	1 cup	250 mL
Chunky salsa	1 cup	250 mL
Brown sugar, packed	1 tsp.	5 mL
Dried basil	1 tsp.	5 mL
Chopped fresh parsley (or 3/4 tsp., 4 mL, flakes)	1 tbsp.	15 mL
Sour cream	1/2 cup	125 mL
Grated Monterey Jack cheese	1/2 cup	125 mL

Heat cooking oil in large frying pan on medium. Add beef, scramble-fry for about 10 minutes until no longer pink. Drain well. Transfer to 5 to 7 quart (5 to 7 L) slow cooker.

Add next 10 ingredients. Stir. Cook, covered, on Low for 8 to 10 hours or on High for 4 to 5 hours until vegetables are tender.

Add parsley. Stir.

Spoon sour cream and sprinkle cheese on individual servings. Makes about 14 cups (3.5 L).

1 cup (250 mL): 281 Calories; 7.1 g Total Fat (2.2 g Mono, 1.0 g Poly, 3.0 g Sat); 26 mg Cholesterol; 37 g Carbohydrate; 7 g Fibre; 19 g Protein; 581 mg Sodium

Pictured on page 125.

Hurried Hamburger Soup

Mild flavours reminiscent of the familiar hamburger noodle casserole.
Just as comforting in soup form, it's on the table in about 30 minutes.

Cooking oil	1 tsp.	5 mL
Lean ground beef	1 lb.	454 g
Chopped onion	1 cup	250 mL
Beef stock	5 cups	1.25 L
Can of mixed beans, rinsed and drained	19 oz.	540 mL
Can of diced tomatoes (with juice)	14 oz.	398 mL
Coleslaw mix	1 cup	250 mL
Elbow macaroni	1/2 cup	125 mL
Chili powder	1 tsp.	5 mL
Garlic powder	1/2 tsp.	2 mL
Pepper	1/2 tsp.	2 mL

Heat cooking oil in Dutch oven or large pot on medium. Add beef
and onion. Scramble-fry for about 10 minutes until beef is no longer
pink. Drain.

Add remaining 8 ingredients. Stir. Bring to a boil. Reduce heat to medium.
Simmer, partially covered, for 10 to 15 minutes, stirring occasionally, until
macaroni is tender. Makes about 10 cups (2.5 L).

1 cup (250 mL): 155 Calories; 4.9 g Total Fat (2.1 g Mono, 0.5 g Poly, 1.6 g Sat); 23 mg Cholesterol;
14 g Carbohydrate; 2 g Fibre; 13 g Protein; 576 mg Sodium

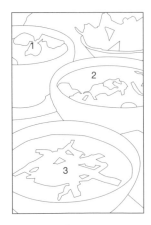

1. Chipotle Chicken Fiesta, page 148
2. Tex-Mex Taco Soup, page 123
3. Mexican Citrus Soup, page 20

Props courtesy of: Canhome Global

Speedy Succotash Soup

You'll be the belle of the ball when you ladle up this high-protein soup based on a favourite dish of the American South. Serve with fresh cheese buns.

Cooking oil	2 tsp.	10 mL
Chopped carrot	1 cup	250 mL
Diced, peeled sweet potato (or yam)	1 cup	250 mL
Chopped onion	1/2 cup	125 mL
Garlic clove, minced (or 1/4 tsp., 1 mL, powder)	1	1
Vegetable (or chicken) stock	5 cups	1.25 L
Bag of frozen lima beans	10 oz.	300 g
Frozen kernel corn	1 cup	250 mL
Dried thyme	1 tsp.	5 mL
Chili powder	1/2 tsp.	2 mL
Salt	1/2 tsp.	2 mL
Pepper	1/4 tsp.	1 mL

Heat cooking oil in large saucepan on medium. Add next 4 ingredients. Cook for about 5 to 10 minutes, stirring often, until onion is softened.

Add remaining 7 ingredients. Stir. Bring to a boil. Reduce heat to medium-low. Simmer, covered, for about 15 minutes, stirring occasionally, until sweet potato is tender. Makes about 7 cups (1.75 L).

1 cup (250 mL): 140 Calories; 2.2 g Total Fat (0.9 g Mono, 0.6 g Poly, 0.5 g Sat); 0 mg Cholesterol; 26 g Carbohydrate; 4 g Fibre; 6 g Protein; 826 mg Sodium

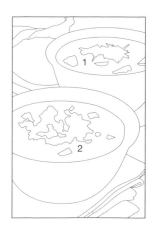

1. Pasta e Fagioli, page 48
2. Lemon Lentil Soup, page 110

Props courtesy of: Pier 1 Imports

Mealtime Minestrone

Our version of minestrone, literally translated as "big soup" in Italian, sure lives up to its name. Consider this big soup to be a big supper treat for any vegetarian or vegetable-loving friends you may have.

Dried chickpeas (garbanzo beans)	1/2 cup	125 mL
Dried red kidney beans	1/2 cup	125 mL
Olive (or cooking) oil	1 tbsp.	15 mL
Finely chopped onion	1/2 cup	125 mL
Finely chopped celery	1/2 cup	125 mL
Finely chopped carrot	1/2 cup	125 mL
Garlic clove, minced (or 1/4 tsp., 1 mL, powder)	1	1
Water	10 cups	2.5 L
Bay leaf	1	1
Chopped cabbage	1 cup	250 mL
Chopped onion	1/3 cup	75 mL
Sliced celery	1/3 cup	75 mL
Sliced baby carrot	1/3 cup	75 mL
Diced red pepper	1/3 cup	75 mL
Pearl barley	1/4 cup	60 mL
Tomato paste (see Tip, page 49)	1/4 cup	60 mL
Parsley flakes	1 tbsp.	15 mL
Dried oregano	1 1/2 tsp.	7 mL
Dried basil	1 1/2 tsp.	7 mL
Cans of stewed tomatoes (with juice), (14 oz., 398 mL, each), chopped	2	2
Ditali pasta (or elbow macaroni)	1/2 cup	125 mL
Salt	1/2 tsp.	2 mL
Grated Parmesan cheese	1/4 cup	60 mL

Measure chickpeas and kidney beans into large bowl. Add water until 2 inches (5 cm) above beans. Let stand for 8 hours or overnight. Drain. Rinse beans. Drain. Set aside.

(continued on next page)

Heat olive oil in large saucepan or Dutch oven on medium. Add next 4 ingredients. Cook for about 10 minutes, stirring occasionally, until vegetables are golden.

Add water, bay leaf and beans. Bring to a boil. Reduce heat to medium-low. Simmer, partially covered, for about 1 hour, stirring occasionally, until beans are almost tender. Discard bay leaf.

Add next 11 ingredients. Stir. Bring to a boil. Reduce heat to medium-low. Simmer, partially covered, for about 55 minutes, stirring occasionally, until vegetables and barley are tender.

Add pasta and salt. Stir. Boil gently, uncovered, for about 15 minutes, stirring occasionally, until pasta is tender but firm and soup is slightly thickened.

Sprinkle individual servings with Parmesan cheese. Makes about 10 cups (2.5 L).

1 cup (250 mL): 179 Calories; 3.4 g Total Fat (1.5 g Mono, 0.7 g Poly, 0.9 g Sat); 2 mg Cholesterol; 31 g Carbohydrate; 5 g Fibre; 8 g Protein; 429 mg Sodium

Paré Pointer

If you carry a chip on your shoulder
it means there is wood further up.

European Sauerkraut Soupreme

Smoked meat, potatoes and sauerkraut will have you hearkening back to the old country. The slow cooker method really brings out the caraway flavour.

Cooking oil	1 tsp.	5 mL
Chopped onion	1 cup	250 mL
Chicken stock	6 cups	1.5 L
Coarsely grated peeled potato	3 cups	750 mL
Diced carrot	1 cup	250 mL
Caraway seed	1/4 tsp.	1 mL
Salt	1/4 tsp.	1 mL
Pepper	1/8 tsp.	0.5 mL
FLAVOUR BOUQUET GARNI		
Garlic clove, halved	1	1
Pickling spice	1 tsp.	5 mL
Bay leaf	1	1
Smoked turkey drumstick	10 – 12 oz.	285 – 340 g
Sauerkraut, drained	2 cups	500 mL
Sour cream	1/2 cup	125 mL

Heat cooking oil in medium frying pan on medium-high. Add onion. Heat and stir for 5 to 10 minutes until starting to brown. Transfer to 4 to 5 quart (4 to 5 L) slow cooker.

Add next 6 ingredients. Stir.

Flavour Bouquet Garni: Place first 3 ingredients on 10 inch (25 cm) square piece of cheesecloth. Draw up corners and tie with butcher's string. Submerge in liquid in slow cooker.

Add turkey drumstick. Cook, covered, on Low for about 8 hours or on High for about 4 hours until meat is falling off bone. Discard bouquet garni. Remove drumstick to cutting board. Remove turkey from bones. Discard skin and bones. Chop turkey into 1/2 inch (12 mm) pieces. Return to slow cooker.

Add sauerkraut. Cook, covered, on High for about 15 minutes until heated through. Makes about 9 cups (2.25 L).

Spoon sour cream onto individual servings. Serves 6.

(continued on next page)

1 serving: 205 Calories; 6.4 g Total Fat (1.7 g Mono, 1.1 g Poly, 3.0 g Sat); 30 mg Cholesterol; 26 g Carbohydrate; 4.5 g Fibre; 13 g Protein; 1922 mg Sodium

Beef Bourguignon Soup

Fine French cuisine in an easy-to-make soup. Red wine, mushrooms and tender beef—your friends and family will swear you studied at Le Cordon Bleu!

Cooking oil	1 tsp.	5 mL
Extra-lean ground beef	1 lb.	454 g
Chopped onion	1 1/2 cups	375 mL
Garlic cloves, minced (or 1/2 tsp., 2 mL, powder)	2	2
Fresh whole white mushrooms, quartered	3 cups	750 mL
Sliced celery	1 cup	250 mL
Dried basil	1/2 tsp.	2 mL
Dried thyme	1/2 tsp.	2 mL
Pepper	1/4 tsp.	1 mL
Bay leaf	1	1
Dry (or alcohol-free) red wine	1/3 cup	75 mL
Beef stock	3 cups	750 mL
Tomato paste (see Tip, page 49)	3 tbsp.	50 mL
Granulated sugar	1 tsp.	5 mL
Salt	1/2 tsp.	2 mL

Chopped fresh parsley, for garnish

Heat cooking oil in large saucepan on medium. Add next 3 ingredients. Scramble-fry for about 10 minutes until onion is softened and beef is no longer pink.

Add next 6 ingredients. Cook for about 5 minutes, stirring often, until mushrooms release liquid.

Add wine. Heat and stir for 1 minute.

Add next 4 ingredients. Stir. Bring to a boil. Reduce heat to medium-low. Simmer, partially covered, for about 10 minutes until celery is softened. Discard bay leaf. Makes about 7 cups (1.75 L).

Garnish individual servings with parsley. Serves 4.

1 serving: 273 Calories; 11.4 g Total Fat (5.0 g Mono, 0.9 g Poly, 4.0 g Sat); 57 mg Cholesterol; 14 g Carbohydrate; 3 g Fibre; 25 g Protein; 1027 mg Sodium

Beef Pho

Experience the authentic tastes of Vietnamese noodle soup.

Partially frozen beef strip loin steak	4 oz.	113 g
Beef stock	6 cups	1.5 L
Water	2 cups	500 mL
Sliced onion	1 cup	250 mL
Lemon grass, bulb only (root and stalk removed)	1/2	1/2
Fish sauce	1 tbsp.	15 mL
Brown sugar, packed	1 tbsp.	15 mL
Star anise	2	2
Piece of ginger root, (1/2 inch, 12 mm, length)	1	1
Dried crushed chilies	1/2 tsp.	2 mL
Salt	1/2 tsp.	2 mL
Package of medium rice stick noodles (Banh Pho), broken	8 oz.	225 g
Thinly sliced onion	1/3 cup	75 mL
Fresh bean sprouts	2 cups	500 mL
Lime juice	2 tbsp.	30 mL
Chopped fresh basil	2 tbsp.	30 mL
Chopped fresh mint	2 tbsp.	30 mL

Lime wedges, for garnish

Slice steak across the grain into short, paper-thin slices. Set aside to thaw.

Combine next 10 ingredients in large saucepan on medium. Bring to a boil. Reduce heat to medium-low. Simmer for about 15 minutes until onion is softened. Strain through sieve into large bowl. Discard solids. Return to saucepan. Bring to a boil.

Add noodles and second amount of onion. Boil gently, uncovered, on medium for about 10 minutes until noodles are softened.

Add next 4 ingredients and beef. Heat and stir for 3 to 5 minutes until beef is no longer pink. Makes about 8 cups (2 L).

Garnish individual servings with lime wedges. Serves 4.

1 serving: 357 Calories; 5.4 g Total Fat (2.0 g Mono, 0.2 g Poly, 1.9 g Sat); 15 mg Cholesterol; 59 g Carbohydrate; 2 g Fibre; 17 g Protein; 1849 mg Sodium

Thai Curried Chicken Soup

This slow cooker soup with green curry paste and coconut milk will have you fit to be Thai-ed. Garnish with cilantro and lime zest.

Cooking oil	2 tsp.	10 mL
Boneless, skinless chicken breast halves, cut into short, thin slices	1 lb.	454 g
Cooking oil	2 tsp.	10 mL
Chopped onion	2 cups	500 mL
Finely grated ginger root	2 tsp.	10 mL
Green curry paste	2 tsp.	10 mL
Chicken stock	6 cups	1.5 L
Small fresh whole white mushrooms, quartered	3 cups	750 mL
Thinly sliced carrot	2 cups	500 mL
Snow peas, trimmed and halved crosswise	2 cups	500 mL
Cooked jasmine rice (about 2/3 cup, 150 mL, uncooked)	2 cups	500 mL
Can of coconut milk	14 oz.	398 mL
Can of bamboo shoots, drained and julienned (see Note)	8 oz.	227 mL

Heat first amount of cooking oil in large frying pan on medium. Add chicken. Cook for about 10 minutes, stirring occasionally, until browned. Transfer to 5 to 7 quart (5 to 7 L) slow cooker.

Add second amount of cooking oil to same frying pan. Add onion. Cook for 5 to 10 minutes, stirring often, until softened. Add ginger and curry paste. Heat and stir for 1 minute. Add to slow cooker.

Add next 3 ingredients. Stir. Cook, covered, on Low for 8 hours or on High for 4 hours.

Add remaining 4 ingredients. Stir well. Cook, covered, on High for 15 to 20 minutes until peas are tender-crisp and rice is heated through. Makes about 13 1/2 cups (3.4 L). Serves 8.

1 serving: 434 Calories; 15.0 g Total Fat (2.4 g Mono, 1.4 g Poly, 10.0 g Sat); 33 mg Cholesterol; 55 g Carbohydrate; 4 g Fibre; 21 g Protein; 685 mg Sodium

Note: To julienne, cut into very thin strips that resemble matchsticks.

Hot And Sour Szechuan Soup

Forget the takeout—here's all the Szechuan flavours you need. Find the Szechuan peppercorns in the Asian section of most large grocery stores.

Chinese dried mushrooms	5	5
Boiling water	1 cup	250 mL
Chicken stock	5 cups	1.25 L
Boneless, skinless chicken breast halves	6 oz.	170 g
Whole black (or Szechuan) peppercorns	1/2 tsp.	2 mL
Can of bamboo shoots, drained	8 oz.	227 mL
Can of sliced water chestnuts, drained and coarsely chopped	8 oz.	227 mL
Firm tofu, cut into 1/2 inch (12 mm) pieces	1/3 lb.	150 g
Grated carrot	1/2 cup	125 mL
Rice vinegar	3 tbsp.	50 mL
Soy sauce	2 tbsp.	30 mL
Chili paste (sambal oelek)	1 tbsp.	15 mL
Finely grated ginger root	1 tbsp.	15 mL
Fresh (or frozen) peas	1/2 cup	125 mL
Sesame oil (optional)	1 tsp.	5 mL
Large eggs, fork-beaten	2	2
Cornstarch	2 tbsp.	30 mL
Chopped green onion	1/4 cup	60 mL

Put mushrooms in small heatproof bowl. Add boiling water. Stir. Let stand for about 20 minutes until softened. Strain through sieve into separate small bowl. Reserve mushroom liquid. Remove and discard stems. Slice thinly. Set aside.

Combine next 3 ingredients in large saucepan. Bring to a boil. Reduce heat to medium-low. Simmer, partially covered, for about 15 minutes, stirring occasionally, until chicken is no longer pink inside. Remove chicken to cutting board. Finely shred chicken. Strain stock. Discard peppercorns. Return chicken and stock to same saucepan.

Add next 8 ingredients. Add mushrooms. Bring to a boil.

Reduce heat to medium. Add peas and sesame oil. Stir. Add eggs slowly in thin stream, stirring constantly, until fine egg threads form.

(continued on next page)

Stir reserved mushroom liquid into cornstarch in small cup. Add to saucepan. Heat and stir for about 1 minute until boiling and thickened. Makes about 8 cups (2 L).

Sprinkle green onion on individual servings. Serves 4.

1 serving: 262 Calories; 8.5 g Total Fat (2.3 g Mono, 2.9 g Poly, 2.3 g Sat); 132 mg Cholesterol; 24 g Carbohydrate; 3 g Fibre; 24 g Protein; 1674 mg Sodium

Pictured on page 35.

Sausage-Fry Soup

The spicy sausage melds perfectly with the cabbage-like flavour of kale.

Cooking oil	1 tbsp.	15 mL
Hot Italian sausage, casings removed, chopped	1 lb.	454 g
Chopped onion	1 1/2 cups	375 mL
Garlic clove, minced (or 1/4 tsp., 1 mL, powder)	1	1
Baby potatoes, quartered	2 lbs.	900 g
Balsamic vinegar	3 tbsp.	50 mL
Dried rosemary, crushed	1/2 tsp.	2 mL
Salt	1/2 tsp.	2 mL
Pepper	1/4 tsp.	1 mL
Bay leaf	1	1
Chicken stock	8 cups	2 L
Chopped kale leaves, lightly packed	3 cups	750 mL

Heat cooking oil in Dutch oven or large pot on medium. Add next 3 ingredients. Scramble-fry for about 15 minutes until onion is softened and sausage is browned. Drain.

Add next 6 ingredients. Heat and stir for 2 minutes, scraping any brown bits from bottom of pot.

Add stock. Stir. Bring to a boil. Reduce heat to medium-low. Simmer, covered, for 15 to 20 minutes, stirring occasionally, until potato is tender. Discard bay leaf.

Add kale. Stir. Cook for about 5 minutes until kale is softened. Makes about 13 cups (3.25 L). Serves 8.

1 serving: 228 Calories; 9.4 g Total Fat (4.2 g Mono, 1.6 g Poly, 3.1 g Sat); 21 mg Cholesterol; 27 g Carbohydrate; 3 g Fibre; 11 g Protein; 1273 mg Sodium

Turkey Spinach Gumbo

*Ma cher amio, this bayou favourite will have you
two-steppin' to the zydeco music all night long! Especially
since the slow cooker will be doing all the work.*

Turkey drumsticks, skin removed (about 2 lbs., 900 g)	2	2
Garlic ham sausage, cut into 1/2 inch (12 mm) thick slices	1 lb.	454 g
Frozen (or fresh) okra, cut into 1/2 inch (12 mm) pieces	2 cups	500 mL
Cooking oil	1/3 cup	75 mL
All-purpose flour	1/3 cup	75 mL
Chopped onion	1 cup	250 mL
Chopped celery	1 cup	250 mL
Chopped green pepper	1 cup	250 mL
Garlic cloves, minced (or 1/2 tsp., 2 mL, powder)	2	2
Dried basil	1/2 tsp.	2 mL
Dried thyme	1/2 tsp.	2 mL
Salt	1/4 tsp.	1 mL
Pepper	1/2 tsp.	2 mL
Cayenne pepper	1/4 tsp.	1 mL
Water	1 1/2 cups	375 mL
Can of condensed chicken broth (see Note)	10 oz.	284 mL
Hot pepper sauce	1 – 2 tbsp.	15 – 30 mL
Cooked long grain white rice (about 2/3 cup, 150 mL, uncooked)	1 1/2 cups	375 mL
Box of frozen chopped spinach, thawed and squeezed dry	10 oz.	300 mL

Put first 3 ingredients into 4 to 5 quart (4 to 5 L) slow cooker.

Heat cooking oil in large frying pan on medium. Add flour. Heat and stir for 5 to 10 minutes until roux is browned (see Thickening Tricks, page 9).

(continued on next page)

Add next 9 ingredients. Stir.

Add next 3 ingredients. Cook and stir for about 5 minutes until boiling and slightly thickened. Add to turkey mixture. Stir. Cook, covered, on Low for 8 to 10 hours or on High for 4 to 5 hours. Remove drumsticks to cutting board using slotted spoon. Remove turkey from bones. Discard bones. Chop turkey. Return to slow cooker.

Add rice and spinach. Stir. Cook, covered, on High for about 5 minutes until heated through. Makes about 11 cups (2.75 L). Serves 6.

1 serving: 515 Calories; 25.0 g Total Fat (8.4 g Mono, 4.8 g Poly, 2.0 g Sat); 77 mg Cholesterol; 33 g Carbohydrate; 4 g Fibre; 38 g Protein; 1241 mg Sodium

Pictured on page 144.

Note: If preferred, substitute 2 3/4 cups chicken stock for condensed chicken broth and water.

 To make soured milk, measure 1 tbsp. (15 mL) white vinegar or lemon juice into a 1 cup (250 mL) liquid measure. Add enough milk to make 1 cup (250 mL). Stir. Let stand for 1 minute.

Chicken And Dumpling Soup

Without our slow cookers we'd certainly swoon! This traditional Southern fave, in soup form, will leave all the beaus and belles feeling satisfied.

Chopped onion	1/2 cup	125 mL
Chopped peeled potato	1 cup	250 mL
Chopped carrot	1 cup	250 mL
Shredded green cabbage, lightly packed	1 cup	250 mL
Small fresh whole white mushrooms, halved	1 cup	250 mL
Boneless, skinless chicken thighs, cut into 1 inch (2.5 cm) pieces	1 lb.	454 g
Chicken stock	2 cups	500 mL
Can of condensed cream of mushroom soup	10 oz.	284 mL
Dried rosemary, crushed	1/4 tsp.	1 mL
Dried thyme	1/4 tsp.	1 mL
Paprika	1/4 tsp.	1 mL
Pepper	1/4 tsp.	1 mL
Bay leaf	1	1
ROSEMARY DUMPLINGS		
All-purpose flour	1 cup	250 mL
Grated Parmesan cheese	2 tbsp.	30 mL
Baking powder	1 tsp.	5 mL
Dried rosemary, crushed	1/8 tsp.	0.5 mL
Large egg, fork-beaten	1	1
Buttermilk (or soured milk, see Tip, page 137)	3 tbsp.	50 mL
Cooking oil	2 tbsp.	30 mL

Layer first 6 ingredients, in order given, in 3 1/2 to 4 quart (3.4 to 5 L) slow cooker.

Combine next 6 ingredients in small bowl. Pour over chicken.

Add bay leaf. Do not stir. Cook, covered, on Low for 6 hours or on High for 3 hours. Discard bay leaf. Stir. Turn temperature to High to allow soup to come to a boil before adding dumplings. Makes 6 cups (1.5 L).

Rosemary Dumplings: Combine first 4 ingredients in medium bowl. Make a well in centre.

(continued on next page)

Combine remaining 3 ingredients in small bowl. Add to well. Stir until just moistened. Spoon mounds of batter, using 1 tbsp. (15 mL) for each, in single layer on top of soup. Cook, covered, on High for about 30 minutes until wooden pick inserted in centre of dumpling comes out clean. Serves 6.

1 serving: 344 Calories; 13.8 g Total Fat (5.0 g Mono, 4.3 g Poly, 3.1 g Sat); 99 mg Cholesterol; 32 g Carbohydrate; 3 g Fibre; 22 g Protein; 900 mg Sodium

Chicken Basil Souper

So chock full of chicken there isn't a thing you'll be missin'. Rosy golden broth surrounds a bounty of vegetables. Quick and easy to prepare.

Cooking oil	1 tbsp.	15 mL
Boneless, skinless chicken thighs, chopped	3/4 lb.	340 g
Chopped onion	1 cup	250 mL
Chopped carrot	1 cup	250 mL
Chopped green pepper	1 cup	250 mL
All-purpose flour	2 tbsp.	30 mL
Chicken stock	4 cups	1 L
Can of diced tomatoes (with juice)	14 oz.	398 mL
Bacon slices, cooked crisp and crumbled	4	4
Pepper	1/4 tsp.	1 mL
Chopped fresh basil	3 tbsp.	50 mL
Chopped fresh parsley	2 tbsp.	30 mL
Grated Parmesan cheese (optional)	3 tbsp.	50 mL

Heat cooking oil in large saucepan on medium-high. Add next 4 ingredients. Cook for 5 to 10 minutes, stirring often, until onion is softened.

Add flour. Heat and stir for 1 minute.

Slowly add 1 cup (250 mL) stock. Heat and stir until mixture is boiling and slightly thickened. Add remaining stock. Stir.

Add next 3 ingredients. Stir. Bring to a boil. Reduce heat to medium-low. Simmer, covered, for 15 to 20 minutes, stirring occasionally, until vegetables are tender.

Stir in basil and parsley. Makes about 8 cups (2 L).

Sprinkle Parmesan cheese on individual servings. Serves 4.

1 serving: 275 Calories; 12.2 g Total Fat (5.0 g Mono, 2.8 g Poly, 3.1 g Sat); 76 mg Cholesterol; 20 g Carbohydrate; 3 g Fibre; 23 g Protein; 1154 mg Sodium

Pot Roast Soup

Why wait until Sunday for a pot roast dinner? This rich, stew-like soup with tender meat and vegetables will bring that feeling of savoury Sunday night satisfaction to any day of the week.

Cooking oil	2 tsp.	10 mL
Beef top sirloin steak, trimmed of fat and diced	1 lb.	454 g
Chopped onion	1 cup	250 mL
Garlic cloves, minced (or 1/2 tsp., 2 mL, powder)	2	2
Beef stock	5 cups	1.25 L
Cubed peeled potato	2 cups	500 mL
Baby carrots, halved	1 cup	250 mL
Tomato paste (see Tip, page 49)	1 tbsp.	15 mL
Worcestershire sauce	1 tbsp.	15 mL
Dried thyme	1/4 tsp.	1 mL
Salt	1/4 tsp.	1 mL
Water	1/4 cup	60 mL
All-purpose flour	1/4 cup	60 mL
Frozen peas	1 cup	250 mL

Heat cooking oil in large saucepan on medium-high. Add beef. Cook for about 10 minutes, stirring often, until browned. Reduce heat to medium. Add onion and garlic. Cook for 3 to 5 minutes, stirring occasionally, until onion is softened.

Add stock. Stir. Bring to a boil. Reduce heat to medium-low. Simmer, partially covered, for about 40 minutes until beef is tender.

Add next 6 ingredients. Bring to a boil.

Stir water into flour in small bowl until smooth. Slowly add to soup, stirring constantly, until boiling and thickened. Reduce heat to medium. Boil gently, covered, for 15 to 20 minutes, stirring occasionally, until vegetables are tender.

Add peas. Heat and stir for 3 to 5 minutes until peas are tender. Makes 8 cups (2 L). Serves 6.

1 serving: 233 Calories; 4.8 g Total Fat (2.1 g Mono, 0.7 g Poly, 1.2 g Sat); 36 mg Cholesterol; 24 g Carbohydrate; 3 g Fibre; 23 g Protein; 931 mg Sodium

Goulash Soup

A "souped-up" version of the Hungarian hit!
In keeping with tradition, serve with sour cream.

All-purpose flour	2 tbsp.	30 mL
Paprika	1 tsp.	5 mL
Pepper	1/2 tsp.	2 mL
Stewing beef, trimmed of fat, cut into 1 inch (2.5 cm) cubes	1 lb.	454 g
Cooking oil	1 tbsp.	15 mL
Chopped onion	1 cup	250 mL
Water	1/4 cup	60 mL
Garlic clove, minced (or 1/4 tsp., 1 mL, powder)	1	1
Beef stock	4 cups	1 L
Caraway seed	1 tsp.	5 mL
Can of diced tomatoes (with juice)	14 oz.	398 mL
Diced carrot	1 cup	250 mL
Diced yellow turnip	1 cup	250 mL
Diced peeled potato	1 cup	250 mL

Measure first 3 ingredients into large resealable plastic bag. Add beef. Seal bag. Toss until coated.

Heat cooking oil in large saucepan on medium-high. Add beef. Heat and stir for 3 to 4 minutes until browned. Reduce heat to medium.

Add next 3 ingredients. Cook for about 5 to 10 minutes, scraping any brown bits from bottom of pan, until onion starts to soften.

Add stock and caraway seed. Bring to a boil. Reduce heat to medium-low. Simmer, partially covered, for about 45 minutes, stirring occasionally, until beef is tender.

Add remaining 4 ingredients. Bring to a boil. Cook, partially covered, for about 30 minutes, stirring occasionally, until vegetables are tender. Makes about 7 1/2 cups (1.9 L). Serves 4.

1 serving: 342 Calories; 12.2 g Total Fat (5.2 g Mono, 1.7 g Poly, 3.3 g Sat); 55 mg Cholesterol; 26 g Carbohydrate; 4 g Fibre; 32 g Protein; 1130 mg Sodium

Pictured on page 143.

Fall Harvest Feast

The colours of fall are reflected in this feast for the eyes—and the stomach!

Bacon slices, chopped	4	4
Boneless, skinless chicken breast halves, chopped	1 lb.	454 g
Chopped onion	1 cup	250 mL
Chopped celery	1/2 cup	125 mL
Chopped carrot	1/2 cup	125 mL
Chicken (or vegetable) stock	1/4 cup	60 mL
Chicken (or vegetable) stock	6 cups	1.5 L
Can of pure pumpkin (no spices)	14 oz.	398 mL
Dried thyme	1/4 tsp.	1 mL
Ground sage	1/8 tsp.	0.5 mL

Cook bacon in large saucepan on medium until crisp. Transfer with slotted spoon to paper towels to drain. Set aside.

Heat 1 tbsp. (15 mL) drippings in same saucepan on medium-high. Add chicken. Cook for about 8 minutes, stirring often, until browned.

Add next 4 ingredients. Heat and stir for about 5 to 10 minutes, scraping any brown bits from bottom of pan, until vegetables are softened.

Add remaining 4 ingredients. Stir. Bring to a boil. Reduce heat to medium-low. Simmer, covered, for about 30 minutes, stirring occasionally, until vegetables are tender. Add bacon. Stir. Makes about 8 1/2 cups (2.1 L). Serves 4.

1 serving: 280 Calories; 9.5 g Total Fat (3.5 g Mono, 1.2 g Poly, 3.9 g Sat); 74 mg Cholesterol; 17 g Carbohydrate; 3 g Fibre; 32 g Protein; 1476 mg Sodium

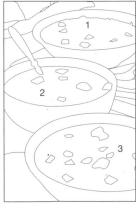

1. Cajun Gumbo, page 146
2. Goulash Soup, page 141
3. Turkey Dinner Soup, page 149

Props courtesy of: Canhome Global
Cherison Enterprises Inc.
Danesco Inc.

Faked Baked Potato Soup

If you like your baked potato with all the fixings, you'll adore this soup.

Cooking oil	1 1/2 tsp.	7 mL
Chopped onion	1/2 cup	125 mL
Diced carrot	1/2 cup	125 mL
Chopped celery	1/2 cup	125 mL
Chicken stock	4 cups	1 L
Diced peeled potato	4 cups	1 L
Dill weed	1/4 tsp.	1 mL
Pepper	1/4 tsp.	1 mL
Bacon slices, cooked crisp and crumbled	**8**	**8**
Grated medium Cheddar cheese	**1/2 cup**	**125 mL**

Heat cooking oil in large saucepan on medium. Add next 3 ingredients. Cook for 5 to 10 minutes, stirring often, until onion is softened.

Add next 4 ingredients. Stir. Bring to a boil. Reduce heat to medium-low. Simmer, uncovered, for 10 to 15 minutes, stirring occasionally, until potato is tender.

Add bacon. Stir. Makes about 8 cups (2 L).

Sprinkle cheese on individual servings. Serves 4.

1 serving: 310 Calories; 13.7 g Total Fat (5.4 g Mono, 1.5 g Poly, 6.0 g Sat); 26 mg Cholesterol; 35 g Carbohydrate; 4 g Fibre; 13 g Protein; 1191 mg Sodium

1. Turkey Spinach Gumbo, page 136
2. Turkey And Bacon Chowder, page 78

Props courtesy of: Emile Henry

Cajun Gumbo

Bring yourself back to the bayou with this fine okra and rice-laden dish.

All-purpose flour	1/3 cup	75 mL
Paprika	2 tsp.	10 mL
Dried thyme	1 tsp.	5 mL
Boneless, skinless chicken breast halves, cut into 3/4 inch (2 cm) cubes	1/2 lb.	225 g
Cooking oil	1/3 cup	75 mL
Diced onion	1 1/2 cups	375 mL
Diced green pepper	1 1/2 cups	375 mL
Diced celery	1 cup	250 mL
Chicken stock	4 cups	1 L
Dry (or alcohol-free) white wine	1/2 cup	125 mL
Can of diced tomatoes (with juice)	14 oz.	398 mL
Package of frozen okra, thawed and cut into 1/2 inch (12 mm) pieces	8 1/2 oz.	250 g
Smoked sausage, chopped	6 oz.	170 g
Long grain white rice	1/2 cup	125 mL
Bay leaf	1	1
Dried oregano	1 tsp.	5 mL
Salt	1/2 tsp.	2 mL
Pepper	1/4 tsp.	1 mL
Cayenne pepper	1/4 tsp.	1 mL
Frozen uncooked medium shrimp (peeled and deveined), thawed	1/2 lb.	225 g
Hot pepper sauce	1/2 tsp.	2 mL

Combine first 3 ingredients in large resealable plastic bag. Add chicken. Seal bag. Toss until coated. Transfer chicken to large plate. Reserve remaining flour mixture.

Heat cooking oil in Dutch oven or large pot on medium. Add chicken. Cook for about 5 minutes, stirring occasionally, until starting to brown.

Add next 3 ingredients. Stir. Cook for about 5 to 10 minutes, stirring often, until vegetables start to soften. Sprinkle with reserved flour mixture. Heat and stir for 1 minute.

(continued on next page)

Suppertime Soups

Slowly add stock and wine, stirring constantly and scraping any brown bits from bottom of pan until boiling and thickened.

Add next 9 ingredients. Stir. Bring to a boil. Reduce heat to medium-low. Simmer, partially covered, for about 35 minutes, stirring occasionally, until vegetables are very tender. Discard bay leaf.

Add shrimp and hot pepper sauce. Stir. Cook, covered, for 2 to 3 minutes until shrimp turn pink. Makes about 11 cups (2.75 L). Serves 6.

1 serving: 418 Calories; 18.4 g Total Fat (7.9 g Mono, 4.5 g Poly, 1.7 g Sat); 79 mg Cholesterol; 35 g Carbohydrate; 4 g Fibre; 26 g Protein; 1239 mg Sodium

Pictured on page 143.

Vegetable Tortellini Bowl

Tortellini turns this light tomato broth packed with vegetables into a meal.

Cooking oil	1 tbsp.	15 mL
Chopped onion	2 cups	500 mL
Garlic cloves, minced (or 1/2 tsp., 2 mL, powder)	2	2
Chicken stock	12 cups	3 L
Can of diced tomatoes, drained	14 oz.	398 mL
Grated carrot	1 1/2 cups	375 mL
Chopped zucchini (with peel)	1 1/2 cups	375 mL
Chopped yellow or red pepper	1 cup	250 mL
Bay leaves	2	2
Dried rosemary, crushed	1 tsp.	5 mL
Salt	1/4 tsp.	1 mL
Package of fresh beef-filled tortellini	12 1/2 oz.	350 g
Fresh spinach leaves, lightly packed	3 cups	750 mL

Heat cooking oil in Dutch oven or large pot on medium-high. Add onion and garlic. Cook for 5 to 10 minutes, stirring often, until onion is softened.

Add next 8 ingredients. Stir. Bring to a boil.

Add tortellini. Stir. Reduce heat to medium. Boil gently, uncovered, for about 8 minutes, stirring occasionally, until tortellini is tender but firm.

Add spinach. Stir. Cook for about 2 minutes until spinach is wilted. Discard bay leaves. Makes about 15 cups (3.75 L). Serves 8.

1 serving: 235 Calories; 6.8 g Total Fat (1.1 g Mono, 0.7 g Poly, 0.9 g Sat); 15 mg Cholesterol; 36 g Carbohydrate; 3 g Fibre; 10 g Protein; 1602 mg Sodium

Pictured on front cover.

Chipotle Chicken Fiesta

*Avocado, corn chips and chipotle chicken—all the fixings for
a fine fiesta. But,* por favor, *Señors and Señoritas, chipotle peppers
are quite spicy—so if you like lots of heat, use two!*

Cooking oil	2 tbsp.	30 mL
Boneless, skinless chicken breast halves, cut into 3/4 inch (2 cm) pieces	1/2 lb.	225 g
Chopped red onion	1 cup	250 mL
Chopped green pepper	1 cup	250 mL
Garlic cloves, minced (or 1/2 tsp., 2 mL, powder)	2	2
Chicken stock	5 cups	1.25 L
Fresh (or frozen) kernel corn	2 cups	500 mL
Can of diced tomatoes (with juice)	14 oz.	398 mL
Dried oregano	1/2 tsp.	2 mL
Chipotle peppers in adobo sauce, chopped (see Tip, page 149)	1 – 2	1 – 2
Lime juice	2 tbsp.	30 mL
Corn chips	1 1/2 cups	375 mL
Ripe medium avocado, diced	1	1
Grated Monterey Jack cheese	1 cup	250 mL
Chopped fresh cilantro	3 tbsp.	50 mL

Heat cooking oil in large saucepan on medium-high. Add chicken. Cook
for 3 to 5 minutes, stirring often, until starting to brown.

Add next 3 ingredients. Cook for 5 to 10 minutes, stirring often, until
onion is softened.

Add next 5 ingredients. Stir. Bring to a boil. Reduce heat to medium-low.
Simmer, partially covered, for 15 minutes, stirring occasionally, to
blend flavours.

Add lime juice. Stir. Makes about 9 cups (2.25 L).

Sprinkle remaining 4 ingredients on individual servings. Serves 6.

*1 serving: 324 Calories; 18.6 g Total Fat (8.5 g Mono, 3.0 g Poly, 5.8 g Sat); 40 mg Cholesterol;
25 g Carbohydrate; 4 g Fibre; 19 g Protein; 947 mg Sodium*

Pictured on page 125.

Turkey Dinner Soup

*All the best tastes of a turkey dinner, with wild rice
and cranberries, in a slow cooker soup!*

Chicken stock	6 cups	1.5 L
Thinly sliced fresh white mushrooms	1 cup	250 mL
Diced celery	3/4 cup	175 mL
Wild rice	1/2 cup	125 mL
Diced carrot	1/2 cup	125 mL
Diced onion	1/2 cup	125 mL
Minute tapioca	3 tbsp.	50 mL
Bay leaf	1	1
Dried sage	1 tsp.	5 mL
Pepper	1/4 tsp.	1 mL
Boneless, skinless turkey thigh	1/2 lb.	225 g
Dried cranberries	1/3 cup	75 mL
Can of evaporated milk	6 oz.	170 mL

Combine first 10 ingredients in 4 to 5 quart (4 to 5 L) slow cooker. Let stand for 5 minutes to allow tapioca to soften.

Add turkey thigh. Cook, covered, on Low for about 8 hours or on High for about 4 hours until rice is tender and split. Discard bay leaf. Transfer turkey to cutting board using slotted spoon using slotted spoon. Cut into 1/2 inch (12 mm) pieces. Return to slow cooker.

Add cranberries. Stir. Cook, covered, on High for about 15 minutes until cranberries are softened.

Add evaporated milk. Stir. Makes about 8 cups (2 L). Serves 4.

1 serving: 292 Calories; 6.3 g Total Fat (1.5 g Mono, 0.8 g Poly, 3.5 g Sat); 59 mg Cholesterol; 39 g Carbohydrate; 4 g Fibre; 21 g Protein; 1412 mg Sodium

Pictured on page 143.

Variation: Use same amount of chopped sun-dried tomatoes instead of cranberries.

 tip Chipotle chili peppers are smoked jalapeno peppers. Be sure to wash your hands after handling. To store any leftover chipotle chili peppers, divide into recipe-friendly portions and freeze, with sauce, in airtight containers for up to one year.

Measurement Tables

Throughout this book measurements are given in Conventional and Metric measure. To compensate for differences between the two measurements due to rounding, a full metric measure is not always used. The cup used is the standard 8 fluid ounce. Temperature is given in degrees Fahrenheit and Celsius. Baking pan measurements are in inches and centimetres as well as quarts and litres. An exact metric conversion is given below as well as the working equivalent (Metric Standard Measure).

Spoons

Conventional Measure	Metric Exact Conversion Millilitre (mL)	Metric Standard Measure Millilitre (mL)
1/8 teaspoon (tsp.)	0.6 mL	0.5 mL
1/4 teaspoon (tsp.)	1.2 mL	1 mL
1/2 teaspoon (tsp.)	2.4 mL	2 mL
1 teaspoon (tsp.)	4.7 mL	5 mL
2 teaspoons (tsp.)	9.4 mL	10 mL
1 tablespoon (tbsp.)	14.2 mL	15 mL

Cups

Conventional Measure	Metric Exact Conversion Millilitre (mL)	Metric Standard Measure Millilitre (mL)
1/4 cup (4 tbsp.)	56.8 mL	60 mL
1/3 cup (5 1/3 tbsp.)	75.6 mL	75 mL
1/2 cup (8 tbsp.)	113.7 mL	125 mL
2/3 cup (10 2/3 tbsp.)	151.2 mL	150 mL
3/4 cup (12 tbsp.)	170.5 mL	175 mL
1 cup (16 tbsp.)	227.3 mL	250 mL
4 1/2 cups	1022.9 mL	1000 mL (1 L)

Dry Measurements

Conventional Measure Ounces (oz.)	Metric Exact Conversion Grams (g)	Metric Standard Measure Grams (g)
1 oz.	28.3 g	28 g
2 oz.	56.7 g	57 g
3 oz.	85.0 g	85 g
4 oz.	113.4 g	125 g
5 oz.	141.7 g	140 g
6 oz.	170.1 g	170 g
7 oz.	198.4 g	200 g
8 oz.	226.8 g	250 g
16 oz.	453.6 g	500 g
32 oz.	907.2 g	1000 g (1 kg)

Oven Temperatures

Fahrenheit (°F)	Celsius (°C)
175°	80°
200°	95°
225°	110°
250°	120°
275°	140°
300°	150°
325°	160°
350°	175°
375°	190°
400°	205°
425°	220°
450°	230°
475°	240°
500°	260°

Pans

Conventional Inches	Metric Centimetres
8x8 inch	20x20 cm
9x9 inch	22x22 cm
9x13 inch	22x33 cm
10x15 inch	25x38 cm
11x17 inch	28x43 cm
8x2 inch round	20x5 cm
9x2 inch round	22x5 cm
10x4 1/2 inch tube	25x11 cm
8x4x3 inch loaf	20x10x7.5 cm
9x5x3 inch loaf	22x12.5x7.5 cm

Casseroles

CANADA & BRITAIN Standard Size Casserole	Exact Metric Measure	UNITED STATES Standard Size Casserole	Exact Metric Measure
1 qt. (5 cups)	1.13 L	1 qt. (4 cups)	900 mL
1 1/2 qts. (7 1/2 cups)	1.69 L	1 1/2 qts. (6 cups)	1.35 L
2 qts. (10 cups)	2.25 L	2 qts. (8 cups)	1.8 L
2 1/2 qts. (12 1/2 cups)	2.81 L	2 1/2 qts. (10 cups)	2.25 L
3 qts. (15 cups)	3.38 L	3 qts. (12 cups)	2.7 L
4 qts. (20 cups)	4.5 L	4 qts. (16 cups)	3.6 L
5 qts. (25 cups)	5.63 L	5 qts. (20 cups)	4.5 L

Recipe Index

151

152

L

M

155

Recipe Notes

Recipe Notes

Recipe Notes

The Company's Coming Story

Jean Paré (pronounced "jeen PAIR-ee") grew up understanding that the combination of family, friends and home cooking is the best recipe for a good life. From her mother, she learned to appreciate good cooking, while her father praised even her earliest attempts in the kitchen. When Jean left home, she took with her a love of cooking, many family recipes and an intriguing desire to read cookbooks as if they were novels!

„Never share a recipe you wouldn't use yourself."

When her four children had all reached school age, Jean volunteered to cater the 50th anniversary celebration of the Vermilion School of Agriculture, now Lakeland College, in Alberta, Canada. Working out of her home, Jean prepared a dinner for more than 1,000 people, launching a flourishing catering operation that continued for over 18 years. During that time, she had countless opportunities to test new ideas with immediate feedback—resulting in empty plates and contented customers! Whether preparing cocktail sandwiches for a house party or serving a hot meal for 1,500 people, Jean Paré earned a reputation for great food, courteous service and reasonable prices.

As requests for her recipes increased, Jean was often asked the question, "Why don't you write a cookbook?" Jean responded by teaming up with her son, Grant Lovig, in the fall of 1980 to form Company's Coming Publishing Limited. The publication of *150 Delicious Squares* on April 14, 1981 marked the debut of what would soon become one of the world's most popular cookbook series.

The company has grown since those early days when Jean worked from a spare bedroom in her home. Today, she continues to write recipes while working closely with the staff of the Recipe Factory, as the Company's Coming test kitchen is affectionately known.

There she fills the role of mentor, assisting with the development of recipes people most want to use for everyday cooking and easy entertaining. Every Company's Coming recipe is *kitchen-tested* before it is approved for publication.

Jean's daughter, Gail Lovig, is responsible for marketing and distribution, leading a team that includes sales personnel located in major cities across Canada. Company's Coming cookbooks are distributed in Canada, the United States, Australia and other world markets. Bestsellers many times over in English, Company's Coming cookbooks have also been published in French and Spanish.

Familiar and trusted in home kitchens around the world, Company's Coming cookbooks are offered in a variety of formats. Highly regarded as kitchen workbooks, the softcover Original Series, with its lay-flat plastic comb binding, is still a favourite among readers.

Jean Paré's approach to cooking has always called for *quick and easy recipes* using *everyday ingredients*. That view has served her well. The recipient of many awards, including the Queen Elizabeth Golden Jubilee Medal, Jean was appointed Member of the Order of Canada, her country's highest lifetime achievement honour.

Jean continues to gain new supporters by adhering to what she calls The Golden Rule of Cooking: *Never share a recipe you wouldn't use yourself.* It's an approach that has worked—*millions of times over!*